The Detective Novel of Manners

Hedonism, Morality, and the Life of Reason

Hanna Charney

Rutherford • Madison • Teaneck
Fairleigh Dickinson University Press

London and Toronto: Associated University Presses

© 1981 by Associated University Presses, Inc.

Associated University Presses, Inc.
4 Cornwall Drive
East Brunswick, New Jersey 08816

Associated University Presses
69 Fleet Street
London, EC4Y 1EU, England

Associated University Presses
Toronto M5E 1A7, Canada

Library of Congress Cataloging in Publication Data
Charney, Hanna Kurz.
    The detective novel of manners.

    Bibliography: p.
    Includes index.
    1. Detective and mystery stories—History and
criticism. 1. Title.
PN3448.D4C44   809.3'872   79-17634
ISBN 0-8386-3004-9

Printed in the United States of America

The Detective Novel
of Manners

For Maurice

Auf welches Instrument sind wir gespannt?
Und welcher Geiger hat uns in der Hand?
O süsses Lied.

Contents

Preface

This study began in pastoral reflections nourished by the Cobb Memorial Library of Truro, Massachusetts. Since academics like the notion of offshoots, perhaps because of its spurious allusion to organic life, this study is an offshoot twice removed of preoccupations with the contemporary novel, which at one time led me to a minor investigation of parodies of detective fiction in the French New Novel. The temptation quickly followed for me to look more fully at the real thing, the models for these parodies. Thus started what I hope is a lifelong addiction. Although believing firmly, in Mark Twain's phrase, that the reports of the death of the novel were vastly exaggerated, I had to admit that the narrative impulse, seemingly irrepressible in writers as well as in readers, is rather exhausted in much of modern literature. It became clear to me that detective novels are a form of noble protest, to the enjoyment of which I humbly devoted this effort.

Friendly thanks go to Gloria and Don Wiener, who long ago sparked detective interests in the gracious hospitality of their country home. I thank the kindest of neighbors, Margaret Ginsberg, for the many books she has so selflessly pressed me to receive and read. The range and taste of the works supplied me by the Murder Ink. Bookshop, that haven of mystery devotees nestled on West Eighty-Seventh Street in New York City, have made my endeavors more pleasant than they might otherwise have been.

A colleague of mine at Hunter College, Jaime Herszenhorn, who is writing on the Argentinian detective novel, has shared some of his excellent ideas with me and made important bibliographical suggestions. Michael Riffaterre, whose every word counts, encouraged me (inadvertently perhaps) by making kind remarks about my earlier foray into the *roman policier*. Reinhard Kuhn, whose conception of detective fiction is noble and far-reaching, has been helpful and supportive. With her unparalleled erudition, Jeanine Plottel has given me important advice, and Eleanor Bergstein, herself a professional writer, has twice supplied a necessary push at crucial moments. I am immensely grateful to Harry Keyishian and Martin Green, whose expertise and intelligent encouragement have been decisive, as well as to Robin W. Winks for his generous and insightful reading of the manuscript.

With uncanny intuition, my son Leopold has often put me on the right track. He has pointed out comic analogues, given me many treasured books, and insisted with forceful tact that I expand my reading of certain authors. My son Paul has been tolerant of an eccentricity that has often offended his artist's eye, especially when the more reprehensible book covers have desecrated his home. My greatest debt is to my husband Maurice, whose masterful and inimitable example, instead of acting as a deterrent, has been a source of joyful inspiration. His help, from the most specific to the most fundamental, amounts to a collaboration.

Introduction:
New Forms in Old Formats

Michael Holquist teases us with a compelling paradox: "The same people who spent their days with Joyce were reading Agatha Christie at night."[1] Even if takes a diurnal-nocturnal dichotomy to do so, this assertion squarely places detective fiction where it belongs. The yearning for premodern forms, nostalgia for a society that has disappeared, and a sense of history are not the exclusive province of "popular art" with its cast of millions to buttress sociological arguments. Until the 1930s, the novel itself was often seen as a lower genre, and Stendhal wondered how to keep "a pretty woman" reading until the small hours of the morning rather than how to entertain the speculations of critics, theorists, and writers of dissertations.

The English novel of manners — the long narrative flow that carries pictures of a society that never was but only seemed to be — addressed a literary need, which, I believe, is reasserting itself in detective fiction. I venture to use the term "detective novel of manners" to describe a recognizable body of fiction that in some ways recreates the assumptions that were familiar to readers of Anthony Trollope, Jane Austen, George Eliot, and Henry James. Through the distancing of irony and a sharp self-consciousness, and the concern to revive a tradition boldly but without obsolescence, the detective novel has adopted the format of the novel of manners. The detective novel of manners shapes its own society, where understanding of social and moral norms is expected, where crime must be

taken into account, where conventions provide a shorthand for
a morality asserted and reasserted, where distinctions become
a matter of life and death, and where narrators can speak to
readers through the pervasive guise of an accepted fable and
without the intricate guile of a torturous "sincerity."

Our reading of Trollope, and certainly of Austen and
James, has changed. What may have seemed in 1900 or even
in 1925 to be a mimetic presentation of a "real" world is
modulated by critical habits that point to different structures.
Borrowing the term "quasi-mimetic" from Meir Sternberg,[2]
who applies it in an eloquently rigorous sense, I would like to
use it more broadly for a general balance of realities
established in the novel in relation to those conceived as
existing outside it. Trollope's notorious generalizations[3] about
psychological truths function like his often judgmental
portraits of character, which abound in adjectives referring to
their moral qualities and defects ("wicked," "naughty") setting
the norms of the novel. It is ultimately true that, as Chatman
says, Trollope's narrator "is deeply *into* his story, feels dislike
or affection for his characters, and would not for the world
disturb the reader's illusion that there really is 'somewhere,' a
Barchester, with its bishop, dean, archdeacon, prebenderies,
and, of course, their wives" (p. 248). But Trollope's narrator,
self-mocking, tactful, and considerate, maintains a constant
play of precautions with the reader — apologizing for delays in
exposition, apparent inconsistencies, or the necessities of
suspense — and with the characters as well, whose right to
privacy he often amusingly respects.

The illusion depends on the cooperation of reader and
narrator, which seems to interest Henry James almost as much
as it does Trollope, despite the latter's widely different
techniques and ideas. For James too the "cunning reader" is
crucial, when the author "has revelled in the creation of alarm
and suspense and surprise and relief, in all the arts that
practise, with a scruple for nothing but a lapse of application,
on the credulous soul of the candid or, immeasurably better,

on the seasoned spirit of the cunning reader."[4] The readers, treated with careful confidence, become members of a society contiguous with that of the work, and their reactions are partly defined through it. The readers become Stendhal's "Happy Few"; those who are fortunate enough to have found the author who wrote for them.

Symmetrically, among the characters there is a range and a choice. In Jane Austen's *Pride and Prejudice,* as Sternberg shows, "Elizabeth's vision of the world as divided between the simple and the intricate" is *not* also the author's: "For the work precisely demonstrates that such dichotomies, whether psychological or moral, should be turned into continuums or else they will fail to accommodate the variety and complexity of life, even of comically stylized life" (p. 138). Partiality and prejudice in the novel constantly endanger the judgment of character. Errors and misconceptions frequently occur, for any semblance of truth results only from the balancing out of different views. There is an impressive quest for knowledge, according to Sternberg, both in Jane Austen and in the late novels of James, as reflected by "clusters of words . . . drawn from the general semantic field of the characteristically human quest for knowledge" (p. 133). The list of words offered as evidence is equally impressive.

In the novel of manners the quest is through character, and reality is given in its social form. Conflict, philosophical inference, change, and mortality are viewed through the characters' interaction in their given environment. Problems are defined in their relations to the society in which they occur, which is their explicit dimension. The "slice of life" is cut along that layer where mankind communicates, through words and other behavior, within the structure of a given society. Any society of this type has become difficult to isolate and to describe; no homogeneous group, English or otherwise, provides an easy referential model. On the basis of one fundamental agreement, the rejection of crime and, above all, murder, the detective novel of manners recreates—artificially, deliberately, and often parodistically—the social world that is the stage of a particular action.

In an important article, "Murder and Manners: The Formal Detective Novel," George Grella[5] has shown that the detective novel "remains one of the last outposts of the comedy of manners in fiction" (p. 33). In contrast to W. H. Auden's theory of tragic catharsis in detective fiction,[6] Grella says that the comic purpose blends with the functional one: the "posh and pedigreed society . . . offers social forms for the novelist of manners and, within those forms, the observable clues to human behavior by which the detective hero can identify the culprit" (p. 39). One difficulty in Grella's perceptive analyses is that, by a habit which persists even in most recent studies, they are based entirely on the detective fiction of the "Golden Age": the 1920s and 1930s—although sometimes, there is the grudging recognition of a few straggling survivors. This view seriously distorts perspective. Since the "posh and pedigreed society" that figures in many English novels was still in place in the 1920s and 1930s, the confusion between the real world and that of the novel is hopelessly perpetuated. All the social milieus of subsequent works, especially contemporary ones, disappear in the process.

But detective fiction is still alive and well. It is read by many thousands of readers not only in a nostalgic return to a form practiced in the "Golden Age" but also out of a lively interest in the works of authors who are still writing at present. Readers of detective fiction tend to be almost as aware as the authors of moving in a realm whose laws they know and whose population bears a certain family resemblance. The readers may travel with ease from Agatha Christie to Ngaio Marsh or Dorothy Sayers or J. J. Marric, but be conscious of stepping into foreign territory if they follow the tortured quests of Sam Spade, the superhuman exploits of James Bond, or the intricacies of passion in a French *roman policier* of the "Série Noire."

Detective fiction can be understood as a "minor literature."
In *Kafka: Pour une littérature mineure* by Gilles Deleuze and
Félix Guattari, there are extremely interesting suggestions on
this score. A minor literature (in the case of Kafka, but also of
Irish authors, such as Joyce and Beckett) is interpreted as a
revolutionary use of a "major" language by linguistic exiles.
The "major" conventions are kept, but in special ways: "what
is also interesting is the possibility of putting one's own
language, . . . assuming that it is a major language or was
one at one time, to a minor use. To be in one's language like
an alien. . . ."[7] The interplay between the major and the
minor is pervasive in detective fiction and can work in several
ways. The model may be the "great" novel of a period, into
which detective conventions are infused — Michael Innes, for
instance, uses the French New Novel parodistically in *An
Awkward Lie* (1971) — or a detective pattern may leave room
for developments that are proper to the major novel or the
novel of manners. A work may present itself as contemporary
in its conception of character, its views on the police, drugs,
traffic, or cities, and unobtrusively support the detective
pattern of the investigation leading to the discovery of the
criminal. Other novels, through their tone, character
portraits, and organization, echo Victorian fiction in their
general feeling; then, the brutality of the murder becomes the
scandalous dissonance that shatters the social structures. Still
other novels follow a classic detective composition, in which
psychological and social variations are played in a minor key.
How revolutionary this process may be depends on the themes
and on the power of the forms that structure the works. But it
is worth remembering that revolution has various faces (and a
mirror image): in a time of chaos, order can be revolutionary.

Interest in "popular art" in America, "paralittérature" in
France, or "Trivialiteratur" in its German guise, has recently
evoked serious critical concern. In *Adventure, Mystery, and
Romance,* John G. Cawelti proposes the notion of "odd

analogies between the figure of the detective and that of Dr.
Freud, . . . [an analogy] noted in Meyer's delightful *The
Seven-Percent Solution.*"[8] The Freudian detective leads to an
often recurring theme, which Cawelti formulates as the
middle-class nature of detective fiction: "Readers of classical
detective stories, we hypothesize, shared a need for a
temporary release from doubt and guilt, generated at least in
part by the decline of traditional moral and spiritual
authorities, and the rise of new social and intellectual
movements that emphasized the hypocrisy and guilt of
respectable middle-class society" (p. 104). A German study of
Agatha Christie's work by Gerd Egloff[9] systematically tries to
prove the thesis that Christie's detective novels were an
instrument of "socialization," of propaganda, as it were, for
middle-class values.

There is undoubtedly truth in Cawelti's ideas, but what
these ideas may mean specifically is another matter. The
reassurance of the middle class is so vague a principle that it is
almost impossible to evaluate in sociological or historical
terms, not to mention its literary function. One would need to
suppose that "formulaic art," following rules that are different
from literary ones, has special effects on particular segments of
society, or that some social groups seek special reactions in
certain "popular" forms. This view cannot elucidate the
catharsis that the detective novel provides. Some older critics
insisted on a literary interpretation of detective fiction, a need
strongly reasserted in Michael Holquist's study. As soon as we
enter this frame, the hypothetical reader is no longer
extrapolated to represent a whole social class, but represents
instead a way of reading.

The detective novel takes its place in literary history —
mostly by reaction. In his brilliant analyses of the *roman
policier* in 1942, Roger Caillois speculated[10] that the revival of
the detective novel in France in the 1930s constituted a
reaction against the increased openness and looseness of the
other novels of the period. This perspective situates the

detective novel in the context of the "major" novel, which brings to light the novelistic component of detective fiction. The identity of the detective novel has been obscured by its adherence to the tradition of detection and its resemblance to the detective story, in which, since Poe illustrated the dynamics of the form, writers have emphasized and overemphasized the rules that produce the desired effects. The Detection Club of London (founded in 1929) formulated "fair play rules." Monsignor Ronald A. Knox prefaced his "Studies in the Literature of Sherlock Holmes" (in *Essays in Satire*, 1928) with the "Ten Commandments of Detection." S. S. Van Dine went Knox ten better and presented "Twenty Rules for Writing Detective Stories." There is a strong tradition of dogmatic thinking, and even extremely perceptive critics such as Jacques Barzun tend to apply normative and prescriptive standards in discussing works of detection.

In this framework the short story is the model. Barzun, in his Introduction to *The Delights of Detection*,[11] readily admits that, in his view, the novel form diffuses the strength of the detective puzzle, whose elegance of design is best preserved in short and concentrated works. Dorothy Sayers has often been taken to task for the "useless" developments of her longer novels, and although her critical writings on detection have lost little of their interest and validity, they do not take account of the fullness of her own novels, such as *Gaudy Night*. In *The Omnibus of Crime*, Dorothy Sayers's insistence on technical skill and invention (and her ideas on "viewpoint") lag far behind the author's own fictional accomplishments. The detective story has its own unique development, which some critics defend with eloquence. L. A. G. Strong, for example, argues:

No, the crime story need not be short on characterisation. What it must do is keep it under control. It must establish and maintain proportion between character and plot in exactly the same way as it does between narrative and dialogue. Each crime story, like each straight short story, must decide on its centre of gravity. It must be quite clear whether its main strength is in people or in pattern.[12]

The purpose of this study, however, is to consider the detective novel as a distinct entity. It stems from the detective story, at least in theory and structure, if not in its thematic beginnings, which some trace back to the Bible. Many of the elements of the detective novel overlap with the story, and authors vary considerably in their affinities toward one genre or the other. The novels of Agatha Christie, for example, emerge from the short story, whereas more recent writers such as Patricia Moyes or P. D. James are primarily novelists. On one side, the detective novel touches its parent form, the detective story, and on the other side it touches the novel in general. In this situation, midway between the novel and the detective story, we may find the key to the special meanings of the detective novel. It is poised in a dialectic balance mirrored in all the main aspects of its structure, its conception of character, and its moral attitudes.

Evading the siren songs of psychoanalytic and sociological interpretations, this study assumes that the detective novel exists as a separate entity in varied and innovative, but conventionally discernible forms. It relies on certain expectations and fulfills them. It works toward a catharsis that is characteristic of it and that is different from the exorcism offered by adventure stories, spy novels, and other forms of crime fiction. In his crucial study, Régis Messac[13] showed, in 1929, the influence of scientific rationalism on the detective novel. This influence has often been assumed, but has also been disputed and then reaffirmed—all rightly so, I believe, depending on one's point of view. In *Bloodhounds of Heaven*,[14] which traces the character of the detective in English fiction from Godwin to Doyle, Ian Ousby legitimately questions Messac's theory as it applies to his detectives, most of whom predate detective fiction. But scientism undisputably left its mark on Sherlock Holmes and many others. In all likelihood, Poe also hankered for a "potent sense of reason which finds its highest expression in *The Murders in the Rue Morgue* and *The Purloined Letter*."[15]

In the detective novel, some of the rational premises remain fundamental: the postulation of a reality accessible to reason, confidence in order, and authority of the author who guides the action into a "future [that] is fixed," as Dorothy Sayers said. But the conditions and forms of reason, of social order, and of moral reliability have changed together with literary realities. And although the detective novel may be today the most highly structured literary form, it sometimes reflects methods of reasoning that are as far removed from Sherlock Holmes as they are from Bacon or Descartes. The mainspring of the action, however, remains the one stated by Caillois: murder and detection. All the aesthetic exfoliations of the detective novel are rooted in the process of discovery.

This rigorous law of structure has great charm for the modern mind. The detective novel presents a model in which reality can be understood — and partly conquered — in a small sector of given problems, posed on a human scale (and in this respect detective fiction is clearly middle class). This same attempt to delineate the terms of awareness and understanding underlies the New Novels in France, which are strongly inspired by detective fiction. The French critic Ludovic Janvier goes so far as to say that "the New Novel is the detective novel taken seriously."[16] In a study of authors ranging from Balzac and Dickens to Borges and Robbe-Grillet, Arnold L. Weinstein has suggested an "epistemological perspective" in which

all novels are mystery stories, and all novels both describe and engender the acquisition of knowledge. . . . Balzac and Dickens write out of different traditions, and they have different aims; each writer, however, utilizes the mystery form, builds his own work around the effort to penetrate codes, to perceive (and honor) the human bonds obscured by rigid societal norms. Likewise, Faulkner and Bernanos have little in common *except* the effort to tap the affective potential that the forms of ellipsis, mystery, and disorder afford.[17]

If all novels revolve around a mystery, they are nevertheless not all detective novels. What then is a detective novel? According to Auden's lucid formula, the basic plot of the detective story is this: "a murder occurs; many are suspected; all but one suspect, who is the murderer, are eliminated; the murderer is arrested or dies."[18] This beautifully simple description might well define the genre completely, and it leaves conveniently empty spaces in which the novel can find further definitions.

"A murder occurs": this is the beginning, and the verb is well chosen. Nothing leads up to the murder in the province of detection; it occurs inexplicably. There are variants: a death may occur, which later turns out to have been murder. This death is the initial shock that sets the action in motion. Barzun sees this function as almost exclusive: "The reason why murder animates most detective story-telling is that the gravity of the deed gives assured momentum. Crime, moreover, makes plausible the concealment that arouses curiosity."[19] This may be true in the short story, but in the detective novel the murder also establishes the philosophical framework from the start. We are in a social world, where evil is man-made. The question of death is clearly set apart from murder, which is the real problem. The characters' quarrel is with human reality, not with God or nature, or even themselves.

"Many are suspected": this suspicion, necessitated by the investigation, may be purely functional in the detective story, but in the detective novel it draws wide circles. All aspects of psychological presentation take their keynote from this "generalized suspicion," as Ludovic Janvier calls it (p. 46). The author may use a variety of techniques, but a certain distance is always maintained in the view we have of most characters. In a sense, this is the general perspective of the novel of manners. "All but one suspect, who is the murderer, are eliminated": this describes the central process of investigation, of detection itself. It is as fundamental in the detective novel as it is in the detective story, although it may be much more complex. "Eliminated" is an excellent word to indicate the nature of this action. The word "eliminated" has a double meaning, which sometimes applies. Some suspects may indeed by "eliminated" by murder, but this does not necessarily clear them of suspicion. The real "elimination" is a process of reasoning. The detective novel is not so schematic as the detective story, and the suspects are not eliminated one by one. Many suspects are usually exonerated automatically by the discovery of the criminal. But whether the action moves mostly toward clearing suspects, or, more directly, toward finding the murderer, it always takes place on the stage of the mind and the reader follows it there. The murderer is never found by accident (although chance may help). There may be accidents, there may be further murders, but the eventual discovery of the murderer is brought about by the powers of reasoning. There may be more than one murderer, but one crime remains central, and the criminals involved in it are connected in some way. And the result is as clear-cut as Auden's assertions: the murderer or the murderers are the culprits we were looking for, and their guilt, mitigated or not, is unambiguous.

The murderer must die or be arrested. The detective novel ends on this resolution and offers the harmonious parallel of Auden's sentence: "a murder occurs; . . . the murderer is arrested or dies." In the middle, we find the special opportunities of the detective novel, as each work uses the conventions in its own way and for its own meanings. What Auden's sentence leaves out is the active corollary of the passive voice, which may be the most typically novelistic element of all. The detective himself is a crucial figure, through whose mind the action unfolds. His methods, his profession (if he is an amateur), his conception of his role (if he is a policeman), his point of view, his ideas, his tastes, are the psychological and moral background of the whole work. In the detective novel nothing happens in a mechanical progression. There are always human agents at work, who may be more or less efficient and who are certainly not all-powerful. There is no blueprint of the action, but there is a conventional direction to it, which establishes it firmly in its own genre.

The view presented in this study presupposes that the detective novel is a recognizable genre, an assertion that is explored not for purposes of definition, rule setting, exclusion, or judgment, but in order to look for the particular "pleasure of the text," in the words of Roland Barthes, that this literary species brings forth. Here I take issue with Julian Symons, in his history of crime fiction, *Mortal Consequences.*[20] His witty resistance to classification may be caused partly by the rules of detective fiction that have so often replaced criticism. But it seems wrong to consider thrillers, adventure stories, spy stories, and all kinds of crime novels as "fruits [of the same] tree," the tree being "sensational literature" (p. 4).

The detective novel is the opposite of sensational: deliberately, systematically, and inherently. Its emotional effects are distanced in a manifest and self-conscious way, often through parody or through aesthetic analogues. For example, this is how the victim is described by the detective in V. C. Clinton-Baddeley's *My Foe Outstretch'd Beneath the Tree:*

"I know it's inappropriate to say so — but lying there like that under the catalpa tree early in the morning he looked like an illustration to Blake's poem —

In the morning glad I see
My foe outstretch'd beneath the tree." (p. 65)

Those who set rules for the detective story have often banned psychological or sentimental involvements that might detract from the primacy of detection. Whatever the original reasons were, the detective novel is written in a style that subdues sensory effects. Even gruesome anatomical details tend to be given in legal or medical language, or lightly and in passing. The detective novel does not thrill; the thriller thrills. In an excellent study, *The World of the Thriller,* Ralph Harper[21] has sought to explain how and why the thriller does thrill the reader. This study similarly explores the effects of the detective novel.

Some works of the "hard-boiled" American School, by Dashiell Hammett and Raymond Chandler, for example, could illustrate important differences between the thriller and the detective novel. In a classical composition such as *The Maltese Falcon,* the general outline of the plot resembles that of a detective novel. The detective is asked for help, and, as he starts on his quest, one event leads to another, and one character leads to another, as all converge on the mysterious treasure, the Maltese falcon; finally, Sam Spade turns in the seductress, who is the criminal. Although this is a poor account of what happens in the novel, it is difficult to say much more about it; we are not meant to follow the intricacies of the plot. There is the legend — not too difficult to believe — about Faulkner's brief stay in Hollywood while he was writing the script of a movie based on a novel by Chandler. Eventually, Faulkner, the director, and the actors in the movie so desperately lost track of the action that they called in Chandler, who, equally baffled, suggested that they all stop trying to unravel the plot.

The anecdote makes sense as a parable. To come back to *The Maltese Falcon,* its interest is in its psychological, moral, and sensational effects for which the plot is only a thin support. A dialogue — between Spade and Gutman, for example — could be diagrammatically set out like a boxing match, a battle of wits and mainly of wills, from which Spade emerges pale and shaking, but rebelliously triumphant, smashing glasses as he goes. It is with similar emotions of sadistic and heroic triumph that Spade disengages himself from the embraces of Brigid O'Shaughnessy to bring her to justice. It is on such effects that the novel concentrates. This is not to say that the literal plot is in itself important in a detective novel, but, symbolically, detection underlies the structure. The question that runs through the detective novel is something like this: What can a man or a woman do to understand crime and thus bring order back into chaos, as Caillois says? In a work by Chandler or Hammett the question seems to be: How can a man resist and fight crime and, in the process, still enjoy himself in his own bitter way? Will and action are primary here. In detective fiction, as I understand it, action, necessary though it is, is still refracted by the mind.

This reflexive quality opens the detective novel in a number of different directions, all of which lead far from the short story. In the present study, we follow authors who have shaped and developed the forms of the genre, with all its special modern possibilities, since the 1920s — Margery Allingham, Josephine Bell, Robert Bernard, Nicholas Blake, Agatha Christie, V. C. Clinton-Baddeley, Amanda Cross, E. X. Ferrars, Erle Stanley Gardner, Michael Gilbert, Georgette Heyer, Michael Innes, P. D. James, Harry Kemelman, Emma Lathen, Elizabeth Lemarchand, Frances and Richard Lockridge, Ross Macdonald, J. J. Marric, Ngaio Marsh, Patricia Moyes, Maurice Procter, Ruth Rendell, Dorothy L. Sayers, Simenon, Maj Sjöwall and Per Wahlöö, Rex Stout, Phoebe Atwood Taylor, Josephine Tey, Patricia Wentworth, Sara Woods — to name, as the saying goes, only a few. Their pseudonyms are kept intact, since we are dealing with the products of their imagination as presented in their works. The range is wide, although it comprises only certain areas on the historical map of crime fiction. Boundaries shift as we enter the psychological, moral, and philosophical province of the detective novel of manners.

A great variety of social milieus emerge, defined by history, profession, place, nationality, religion, or class. In a vast gallery of portraits, detectives — young, middle-aged, old, married, single, female, male, amateur, or professional — bring their gifts and their special character traits to bear on the realities they confront. Taste, style, and language describe their own patterns. Comfort and the solace of daily life circumscribe a view of normal existence disrupted by the horrors of crime. And all those lives and works and scenes of the Human Comedy perpetuate themselves as open-ended possibilities.

The Detective Novel
of Manners

1 "The Play's the Thing": Self-Conscious Perspectives

Detective novels are often filled with allusions to books. Many characters in detective novels read at every opportunity — before going to sleep in strange or familiar beds, browsing in old bookstores, or riding on the train. This is true even when the amateur detective does not happen to be a professor of English literature (as is Amanda Cross's heroine or Dr. Davie in V. C. Clinton-Baddeley's novel), or a scholar like Harry Kemelman's Rabbi Small, or even a real policeman like P. D. James's Superintendent Dalgliesh, who has written a volume of poetry. Quotations abound at every turn in detective novels, and lines of Shakespeare make epigraphs for numerous chapters. The dedication — or addiction — to literature varies with different authors, characters, and works. As observed later, the intellectual disposition of the detective crystallizes the values that permeate a particular novel. But what is extraordinarily consistent, to the extent of being a hallmark of detective novels in general, is the use of a book in some form — the whole work, or the title, or quotations from it, or the main themes — as a symbolic reference. The book-within-the-book is a recurring principle; sometimes this principle becomes the basis for the construction of the work.

Agatha Christie, who has experimented with so many different forms and formulas, has used this type of composition several times. She has been praised for avoiding prevalent literary affectations and turning instead to popular literature — nursery rhymes can become the basic clue, as is

1

"Sing a Song of Sixpence" in *A Pocketful of Rye*. (S. S. Van Dine also used nursery rhymes in *The Bishop Murder Case*.) Even the alphabet (in *The ABC Murders*, 1936) can serve. Similarly, other writers have used "unliterary" literature. *The Book of Common Prayer*, for example, is the background to *A New Lease of Death* by Ruth Rendell (1967).

Turning against her own originality, Agatha Christie can also be deliberately learned, with a pretentiousness that reflects the amiable pomposity of her Hercule Poirot. In *The Labors of Hercules* (1939), Christie plays ironically on the (always justified) vanity of the diminutive detective with the splendid mustache and the egg-shaped head. In his semiretirement, Poirot has been persuaded to cultivate himself as well as his garden, and to let "time roll back" as he reads about his illustrious namesake, "a celebrated hero who, after his death, was ranked among the gods, and received divine honors" (p. 9). He is quick to state the exemplum: "Yet there was between this Hercule Poirot and the Hercules of classical lore one point of resemblance. Both of them, undoubtedly, had been instrumental in ridding the world of certain pests. Each of them could be described as a benefactor to the society he lived in." So Poirot decides, on this model, to accept twelve more cases as his own twelve labors of Hercules. And the chapters of the novel follow this preordained structure: "The Nemean Lion," "The Lernean Hydra," "The Arcadian Deer," "The Erymanthian Boar," "The Augean Stables," "The Stymphalean Birds," "The Cretan Bull," "The Horses of Diomedes," "The Girdle of Hyppolita," "The Block of Geryon," "The Apples of the Hesperides," and "The Capture of Cerberus."

The construction of this novel in twelve parts is well integrated with the theme. It corresponds to an initial choice by Poirot, which functions as the catalyst of the action. In this sense, *The Labors of Hercules* is more convincing than *The ABC Murders* and other symbolic artifacts by Agatha Christie. But it does remain overly playful and contrived—as contrived as Poirot's painful attempts at "culture," which is definitely not his cup of tea. "For two hours Poirot read diligently, making notes, consulting his slips of paper and his other books of reference." How much more at ease Poirot is while he savors his sweet "sirops," letting his little gray cells work by divine ordinance and in utterly human comfort! Poirot indeed is a rationalist of the old school, at home in his streamlined apartment rather than in the disorderly world of the Greek gods. He is intelligent and sensitive enough, however, to see that he must make the effort to understand this world.

Another example shows how freely the composition of the whole work can flow from the initial concept, a mirror of a reality reflecting, in turn, as in most detective novels, the nature of the detective novel itself. " 'There must be some explanation for the disappearance of the cucumber,' said Miss Murchiston." We are here with Dr. Davie in *My Foe Outstretch'd Beneath the Tree* by V. C. Clinton-Baddeley. In this masterfully composed novel, Dr. Davie, an elderly scholar from Cambridge, has just arrived as guest lecturer at St. Martha's. The principal, Miss Eggar, has shown Dr. Davie into his room for the night. He unpacks his small suitcase, glances at the books on his bedside table, and, after reading the pompous beginning of "a heavy biography of Dame Margaret Dunstable," he picks up "Annabel Champion's latest country-house mystery, *Who's for Murder?*, its glossy jacket displaying a hypodermic syringe mysteriously couched upon a dish of peaches" (p. 8). " 'There must be some explanation for the disappearance of the cucumber,' said Miss Murchiston." Dr. Davie reads this opening sentence with relief. Let us consider it as a linguistic matrix and pursue it to the corners of the novel. It will reappear like a leitmotiv, discreetly but effectively.

The sentence has, first of all, a literal meaning. It is a profession of faith, implicitly endorsed by Dr. Davie, who "preferred Miss Murchiston to Chief Inspector Bainbridge. Miss Murchiston solved her cases by instinct — which was unfair but preferable to all the boring expertise about police procedures." "There *must* be some explanation" is a postulate of detective fiction, a scientific hypothesis, which will reecho later in Dr. Davie's own endeavors. The fact that there must be an explanation does not guarantee that Dr. Davie will find it, and the explanation may lie outside his pattern of reasoning. "There must be a more certain explanation, just as there had to be an explanation for the disappearance of the cucumber," he reassures himself at one point (p. 76). The patterns of discovery keep shifting, just as attention and concentration may be diverted. "However occupied the mind, nobody thinks of one thing exclusively. In the middle of a desperate decision the fly on the window obtrudes itself" (p. 109). In the "kaleidoscope" of the mind, facts may suddenly present different connections. Dr. Davie says to Inspector Mays: "That theory of mine could be absolutely wrong — and yet the tapes and the murder could be connected in some other way" (pp. 128-29). Although, eventually, the pattern does emerge, the murder of the young actor, Andrew, remains ironically outside. The author here boldly uses a red herring, which takes on a perfect thematic congruence. "There *must* be some *explanation*": "must" and "explanation" define each other. There must indeed be an explanation, but of what kind? The murder that has to do with the drug traffic that Dr. Davie and Mays uncover is part of one pattern; the murder of young Andrew had an explanation also, but it lay outside this pattern. "*Some* explanation" becomes important. There is *some* explanation, but it may be fortuitous, arbitrary, highly unaesthetic, and sad.

"There must be some explanation for the *disappearance*": detective fiction starts with a disappearance, a death, a murder, which is a gap in the world. No matter who or what has disappeared, the person or the object was present once and has been removed by violence. Brent, the main victim in this novel, was certainly an unlikable character, but that is not the point. One may have wanted to punch him, as Robbin, his former schoolmate, did with satisfaction, but he only thought he had killed him that way. As almost always happens in detective fiction, the real killer is criminal.

"There must be some explanation for the disappearance of the *cucumber.*" If it is axiomatic that the value of the object that has been destroyed is not the main issue, the object may be a cucumber. Why shouldn't it be? Hercule Poirot tries to devote his time, in some of the novels, to the cultivation of the English marrow, which requires as much love and care as the most beautiful rose. At any rate, Dr. Davie thinks, the English mania for roses amounts to a vice. Why a rose, then? Why not a cucumber? But the comic choice of the object will later find a tragic counterpart in the death of young Andrew, which Dr. Davie takes very seriously. " 'I am deeply distressed about that boy,' he said. 'I dedicate this investigation to him. In an odd sort of way it could be a kind of revenge' " (p. 136). A revenge, perhaps, against the cruel senselessness of murder. The investigation tries to control murder by discovering its formula, in which every element falls into place.

We have explored this leitmotiv-sentence on its literal level (as a statement of truth), and on its analogical level (as it expresses themes of the novel). This sentence is also parodistic—a parody of itself and of the work in which it appears, with "its glossy jacket displaying a hypodermic syringe." It is also a parody of the work that *we* are reading, of which it is a model. The sentence is a cliché, a commonplace of language, thought, or picture. It is analogous to a "label," such as the label of "country mystery," "detective story," "thriller," a notion that evokes the first paragraphs of the novel, in which Miss Eggar and Dr. Davie exchange amused remarks about the fixed category, "red-brick university":

> "You will observe," said Miss Eggar, "that it really is red brick."
> "This jibe about the red-brick university has always bewildered me," said Davie. "My college at Cambridge is

red brick. So is St. John's. So is Trinity great gate. Half
Cambridge is red brick. What's the matter with red brick?"
"It depends," said Miss Eggar, "on the brick." (p. 7)

Loosely translated, this exchange might mean something like
this:

> "I have never understood these jokes about mysteries.
> Prime Ministers read them, Freud read them, half of the
> intelligent population of the world reads them. What's the
> matter with mysteries?"
> "It depends . . . on the mystery."

The novel itself is the proof, which can transform the parody
or the cliché into a meaningful parable.

The playing-out of a parody can be mainly symbolic and
structural (as it is in Clinton-Baddeley), or moral and
psychological. P. D. James makes an extended use of parody in
Unnatural Causes. The victim, Maurice Seton, was a detective
writer whose own manner of death mimics one of the tricks he
was in the habit of using in his thrillers. A picture emerges of
this vain little man, so proud of his hackneyed productions.
There are abundant examples of his style:

> Carruthers pushed aside the bead curtain and entered the
> nightclub. For a moment he stood motionless in the
> doorway, his tall figure elegant as always in the well-cut
> dinner jacket, his cool ironic eyes surveying with a kind of
> disdain the close packed tables, the squalid pseudo-Spanish
> decor, the shabby clientele. So this was the headquarters of
> perhaps the most dangerous gang in Europe! (p. 28)

Other characters tell of Seton's manias and his petty habits, or
give ironically condensed descriptions of him: "Lost, believed
safe. One middle-aged detective writer. Nervous disposition.
Slight build. Narrow nose. Buck teeth. Sparse hair. Prominent
Adam's apple. Finder, please keep" (p. 24).

But as the novel unfolds, the parody is punctured. We see Seton, for example, through the bitter regrets of Celia Calthrop:

> Sitting in front of the dead fire she recalled the second when she had known the truth, and her cheeks burned at the memory. Suddenly he had begun to cry, awkwardly as a child. In that moment all artifice had been forgotten. Only pity remained. She had knelt beside him. . . . (p. 54)

Celia Calthrop herself is portrayed with a good deal of caricature, so that her emotions are refracted by irony. But the character of Seton does step out of the frame of parody, albeit not too far — just enough to let some light fall on certain features by which we all recognize other characters in the novel as well as ourselves.

This process of coming-to-life (or coming-to-death) can be the mainspring of the action in a detective novel. It certainly is in *Falling Star* by Patricia Moyes. Here, the aesthetic analogue is the film rather than the book. The original paradox is similar to the theme of Antonioni's movie *Blow-Up*: the photograph, either blown up or not, can only yield what it already contains. In the novel, death takes place in a scene of a movie that is being shot. The place is

> a derelict tube station on a small branch line which had not been in use for several years. We had arranged to hire it for the scene in which Professor Masterman is pursuing Rosa through London in a vain attempt to find out where she goes in the afternoons — the answer, of course, is a brothel. (p.23)

This parody of a movie sequence turns into nightmare:

> There was the shriek of the train as it came roaring in from the tunnel. There was Bob, flying helter-skelter down the stairs, shouting, reaching the platform, stumbling. There

> was Keith's voice behind me, shouting, "Bob! Stop him, for
> God's sake!"—and a screech of brakes. There was Fiametta
> Fettini screaming hysterically, "I didn't mean it! I swear I
> didn't mean it!" (p. 38)

The hysterical horror of the scene is given a parodic dimension
by the tone of the narrator, Anthony Croombe-Peters, the son
of "Lord Northburn, who, as you probably know, is not only
an eminent judge but the head of one of the richest families in
the land" (p. 15). Pudge, as Anthony is called, is the pompous
innocent of the lot, proud of his levelheadedness and
bewildered by the irony he elicits. After the actor Robert
Meakin had fallen to his death, Pudge says, "I am pleased to
say that it was Sam and I who restored some sort of order and
telephoned for doctors and ambulances—not that it was any
use" (p. 38).

The death of Robert Meakin, however, transcends parody
(as death always does): "he was quite dead." But the scene will
echo later in what turns into a parody—a reversal of the
original transformation of the parody into horror—
engineered by Henry Tibbett to prove his case:

> The clapper fell with its usual sharp click, and the camera
> swung up to focus on Keith, as he came running down the
> stairs. Suddenly, it reminded me horribly of that similar
> retake in the Underground Station. Just as Bob Meakin had
> done, Keith was ramming his spectacles onto his nose as he
> ran downstairs. His arms flailed wildly, trying to find the
> banisters, and failing. For a long moment, he seemed to be
> poised in mid-air. Then he fell. (p. 236)

But all that ensues is a screaming cat fight between two
characters, in which Keith is not badly hurt. Throughout the
novel, models of reality—movie sets, real scenes, and artificial
situations created by the will of the detective or the author—
are fitted into one another and can mutually parody each
other as well as the work in which they take place. At the end,

the novel remains poised on the initial paradox. "The film is safely in the can," and Chief Inspector Tibbett considers this artistic reality very important: "I believe it is a great film, Pudge. I just wish . . . that I had even a rudimentary understanding of what makes people what they are"(p. 254).

The play on the relations between painting, poetry, and literature and "real" life recurs throughout detective fiction. Theater and acting are also often sources of parody, as in *False Scent* by Ngaio Marsh (1960). Interestingly, *Falling Star* introduces into this play of relations special elements of parody that move both ways, into art and into life. From a hackneyed script, sequences full of clichés, hysterical actresses, and criminal directors, comes a great film. Is it worth it? Perhaps so, but paradoxically. Clinton-Baddeley's Dr. Davie of *My Foe Outstretch'd Beneath the Tree* also tends to answer in the affirmative:

> There were water-colours of Florence and Capri and Taormina on the staircase wall. He stayed to look at them, reminded of pictures painted by his great-aunts at the end of the last century. Nothing could ever look as bright, as pretty, and as peaceful as this again. But Aunt May and Aunt Sophy had both died out there of typhoid fever. So who had the better of it? An ancient question without an answer: though in his heart he thought that probably they had. To have arrived in Venice in a boat with tomato-red sails: that would have been worth a risk. (p. 10)

The element of parody is crucial in detective novels, which does not mean that these novels themselves are parodies (at least not the good ones). Detective novels use parody to establish a level of realism midway between symbol and fact. This balance seems to be a basic law of the genre, applied in the use of the book-within-the-book and in other aspects of structure. It is reflected in the presentation of the victim, of other characters, of society, and of all the realities that compose the novel. This balance may explain why critics and lawmakers of the detective story (including Dorothy Sayers, who broke her own rules) banned any serious love interest. It is in part this same balance that seems to require that all effects be distanced and their emotional impact reduced. Writers about the detective story say that, because the process of detection is paramount, all other elements must be secondary to it. In the detective novel, however, this may be only one of the reasons. In many recent works, the inadequacies of detection are painfully clear, and a number of facts fall outside it. Nevertheless, the level of realism remains consistent in spite of the great differences of tone, intent, and meaning among different works. In other words, the rhetorical conventions remain operative.

One explanation may lie in the use of parody. Through the detective conventions, the detective novel may parody itself in its harshest meanings. As Borges put it: "the solution of a mystery is always less impressive than the mystery itself. Mystery has something of the supernatural about it, and even of the divine; its solution, however, is always tainted by sleight of hand" ("Ibn Hakkan al-Bokhari, Dead in His Labyrinth"). The detective novel always provides the sleight of hand, the inevitable ending, aesthetically as satisfying as the end of a musical movement, but as disappointing as the end of all things. The unraveling of the mystery is not allowed to satisfy us for long. It mocks us, just as it mocks itself. "I find life sad," says Dr. Davie on the last page of *My Foe Outstretch'd Beneath the Tree.* And indeed many detectives, amateur or professional, are profoundly melancholy. Lieutenant Shapiro, who appears in some of the novels by Frances and Richard Lockridge; Simenon's Inspector Maigret (sporadically, after a difficult case); Martin Beck in Maj Sjöwall and Per Wahlöö (irremediably, it seems); and many others exhibit this trait, not to mention those fictional detectives who bear the tragic mark of Sam Spade, such as Ross Macdonald's Lew Archer. Although it may have personal causes, the sadness of these sleuths has symbolic overtones. One of its implications must be that, outside the perfected and rational world of the detective novel, no real detective could so artfully set things straight in the end.

2 Symmetries of Time: Historical Paradigms and Their Literary Counterparts

"Que sera, sera,/ Whatever will be, will be." Interpreted in one way, this refrain from Hitchcock's *The Man Who Knew Too Much* gives a clue to the time orientation of detective fiction. As Dorothy Sayers said, the future is fixed, in the sense that we know from the start that "a rough sort of justice," in Henry Tibbett's words, will be done — speaking largely, legal justice. There are possible variations here. Some detectives or police officers, like Maigret, Tibbett, sometimes Poirot, and Superintendent Alleyn (in Ngaio Marsh) are broad-minded and compassionate, and may be quite willing to let petty crimes disappear in the case. Others are sticklers for legality, and still others, like Perry Mason, are sometimes fastidious, but also, to the lay mind, completely unpredictable in what they consider to be honest before the law. But the central crime must be expiated, the murderer must die or be brought to justice. The detectives sometimes feel that the crime they have investigated is less heinous and more understandable than the actions of the victim, yet they must uncover the criminal. Novelists who tamper with that basic law do so at a cost. When their moral uncertainty and ambivalence go too far, their works disintegrate.

"Nothing was, therefore everything is." Poe's account in *Eureka* of the creation of the universe could serve as a metaphor for the structure of the detective novel (as it does for the short story). Everything starts with the arbitrary fact of a death, the absence around which the action will revolve. Here, too, detective fiction announces an important preoccupation of many contemporary novels, which are built around the original nothing, the central zero. This "scandal" of the murder, as Caillois calls it, is what the detective must set out to avenge, so that order can be brought back to replace chaos. This represents the "future" in the novel. The events that unfold in the present are determined by what will be; that is, what should be: the solution of the crime.

The murder, however, remains unalterable. The victim is dead, and not even the greatest genius of a detective can bring the victim back to life. In that sense, the past is fixed. "Whatever will be, will be" might be complemented by another law: "Whatever was, was." " 'Time is,' quoth the Brazen Head; 'time was; time is past' " (Dorothy L. Sayers, *Gaudy Night,* p. 52). The action of the main murder moves against the narrative current, as many critics have noted. Detection goes backwards toward the crime. In this respect, suspense is deflated almost from the beginning, since the worst has already happened. But then, in this art of balances, suspense is restored by a forward motion.

In the imagery of the stories of Poe and Sherlock Holmes, the concepts are mechanistic, as they are in many short stories of the nineteenth and early twentieth centuries. The clue is a piece of the machine; the puzzle is a reality that can be reconstituted. The police method of reconstructing the scene of the crime still remains dominant in many books by Simenon, for example, although Maigret tends to operate by intuition rather than by logic. Agatha Christie is usually credited with being the first to show systematically, in *The ABC Murders* (1936), how the crime goes forward as well as backward. The schematic model here is convincing, as the crimes continue with the relentlessness of the order of the alphabet. The murderer at large presents an active danger to the other characters. Agatha Christie's procedure is now commonly applied. Once or twice in his career, Hercule Poirot is himself threatened, and many detectives of recent novels are constantly endangered. Those who have a wife and children (Superintendent Alleyn in some of the novels, for example) are subject to blackmail and kidnapping.

There is another turn to this idea of the vulnerability of the detective: he may be charged with a crime himself. This is true not only of lawyers who seem to dance on the edge of the law, like Perry Mason (whom the police always eye with suspicion), but also of highly respectable police officers like Henry Tibbett, who, in *Death on the Agenda,* is the prime suspect. This innovation sometimes degenerates into a conventional formula. Sara Woods's Antony Maitland, for example, makes a habit of getting himself into trouble and attracting a murder charge. The solution of the crime can thus become a matter of survival for the detective himself as well as for the rest of society.

In a contemporary detective novel, one can almost assume that there will be more than one death. In the classic for- mulation of the genre, these deaths are related, so that all the threads of detection can be gathered up at the end. Ngaio Marsh presents these final scenes of explanation in which Alleyn, in the fashion of Hercule Poirot, clarifies the con- nections and implications of the plot. But often the occurrence of the crimes does not create a plausible pattern, but rather sets up clusters of events that may or may not be logically related. The relations may be through the person of a criminal character, or through the activities of the detective, or possibly one of his relatives, in some other connection, or through a sequence of events. Or the events may simply share the same literary space of the novel. The red herring of Andrew's death in *My Foe Outstretch'd Beneath the Tree* is used with par- ticular intelligence, because the author emphasizes its thematic relevance. A character is killed by a sex maniac, a character that the detective happened to visit in connection with another crime. The two crimes are contiguous, no more. It is obligatory for the detective's mind to be instructed by reality and to reform its patterns of reasoning with the help of positive or negative evidence.

Simenon is one of the authors who likes to play on the counterpoint of two (or several) events at the same time. *L'Amie de Madame Maigret* (1952) is an extended example, which juxtaposes Maigret's case of the bookbinder who burned a corpse in his stove with Madame Maigret's role in the action. Her role begins fortuitously with an adventure during a visit to her dentist. The intention is interesting, but the execution is disappointing. The meaning never crystallizes. If the connection was not accidental, what was it? And if it was accidental, why was it? This kind of trickery makes the work veer away from detection; it provokes a bewilderment in which the reader can do nothing but follow, open-mouthed, event after event whose causes remain hidden.

There must be an explanation for the disappearance of the cucumber in detective fiction. All the crimes must come to light. But that poses all the problems of "what was" in reality. And this has become a complex question, for which the old analogy of the puzzle is no longer adequate. What was, "was," in the sense that death has occurred. But the detective is not trying to prove that the victim is dead; this is established empirically. From that arbitrary fact detection only takes its departure. And from that moment on the novel becomes a moving structure, reflecting, as all good modern novels do, a whole perspective in motion, or several perspectives. Michel Butor, the French New Novelist and critic, writes eloquently in *L'Emploi du Temps* about the "new dimension" in detective novels. "Not only are characters and their relations transformed under the eyes of the reader, but what one knows of these relations." (p. 161). Butor further explains that "the narration is no longer the simple plane projection . . . of a series of events, but the restoration of their architecture, their space, since they present themselves differently according to the position occupied in relation to them by the detective or the narrator."

There is not, on one side, the murder, and, on the other, a detective looking for clues. There are dramatic units: the detective-with-this-evidence-thinking-about-this-aspect-which-has-just-come-to-light; a character-explaining-his-interpretation-of-a-fact-he-has-just-revealed; the reader-trying-to-evaluate-the-reliability-of-the-character-who-has-just-spoken-and-to-understand-the-reactions-of-the-detective-while-he-spoke, and so forth, in increasing complexity. Dr. Davie gives a succinct impression of the way in which evidence radiates toward the past as well as toward the future:

> "But because he [Andrew] wasn't there I saw that list — and the list led me backwards to Mary Cragg, to Highgate, to Werner: and forwards to Mr. Corke, to Mr. Palermo, and back to Werner. Everything sprang from that list — and of course from your finding the tape at the back of the drawer." (p. 184)

The action goes backward toward the explanation, forward toward the solution. Both movements are combined in the perspective at work at any given moment. Playing on these perspectives is a universal game of detective fiction. As suspicion falls on one character or another, the total interpretation may change. The famous trick of the narrator-criminal in Agatha Christie's *The Murder of Roger Ackroyd* (1926) is a thorough demonstration. But things become more and more complicated as reality becomes more and more relative.

In *Death Has Deep Roots,* Michael Gilbert makes significant use of changing perspectives. The relation between evidence, reality, and interpretation is a major theme. The whole case is transformed because the accused decides to change lawyers. There is no change in fact, but the new lawyers the accused has chosen start from the hypothesis of her possible innocence, which puts all aspects of the case in a new light. Here is some of the defense's reasoning:

"In this case there is a great deal of evidence. Some people might feel, rather too much evidence. The difficulty is to examine such a body of evidence critically and to see what it means.

"Upon the primary point — about the basic fact — there is no dispute. . . .

"I suggest that when you come to examine the evidence critically . . . you will find that it adds to some proposition such as this.

"The prisoner *could* have murdered Major Thoseby. . . ." (p. 168)

After Macrea, the defense counsel, proposes some of his own interpretations, he continues:

"Now don't start saying to yourselves" — Macrea swung round on the jury again — "Oh, that's just a theory. Of course, it's just a theory. But so is the prosecution's case. There is no more and no less evidence for the one than the other." (p. 171)

A crucial element in the case, which is a variant of the problem of theory against theory, clarifies its meaning. In the judge's private chambers, Macrea says:

The alleged motive here turns entirely on the parentage of a dead child. The prosecution says that Major Thoseby was the father. The defense says Lieutenant Julian Wells. That is the matter in a nutshell. Unfortunately, one of these men is dead, the other has disappeared. The child is in a French grave. All ordinary methods, therefore, of proving or disproving this allegation fall to the ground. (p. 190)

As the lawyer says, that is the matter, symbolically, in a nutshell. The child was born and it died. The fact is in the past and buried there. What *is* this fact in the present, however? The defense is bound to say one thing, the prosecution another. The mother knows the facts, but the lawyers, the judge, the jury, and the reader do not. One can only construct a theoretical pattern in which certain pieces of evidence will take their place:

> "Will the truth come out?" . . . .
> "This may shock you," said Macrea. "I was going to say that it didn't seem to me to matter. I think the truth will come out — sometime. I'm fairly confident that Miss Lamartine won't be found guilty. . . . A disagreement seems the most likely. . . .
> "Well, I suppose that will be a sort of a happy ending," said Mr. Rumbold. "But, you know, it won't satisfy me a bit. . . . I want everything to come out. I want the knots untied and the crooked ways made straight. I want Miss Lamartine set free and the murderer hanged."
> "And the moon," said Macrea. "Don't forget the moon."
> (pp. 198-99)

As such, the past is forever lost. The only aspect of the truth that is not out of reach ("the moon") is this dynamic combination of past fact and present inquiry, in the moral perspective of the mind at work (here the lawyer who *believes* that he is right).

This problem is framed in a similar way in Josephine Tey's *The Daughter of Time* (1951), except that here it is isolated. The crime concerns only the past, the mystery of the murders of the princes in the Tower of London, which were supposedly instigated by King Richard III. This novel presents a fascinating experiment. The suspense produced by our interest in the future (the fate of the characters affected by the consequences of the crime or the charge) is missing. It is replaced by our general familiarity with this historical episode and its versions in literature, especially Shakespeare's *Richard III*. As Grant, with the help of a student, investigates the mystery, he concludes that King Henry VII and not King Richard III was guilty of the crimes. This reconstruction of the past, this shifting of focus as in a stereograph image, is made all the more effective by the final irony: the theory is not new. Detection has reconstituted an old theory. The truth remains poised in the present, which has buried the past.

Why then does it matter? The question can be asked about the whole structure of the detective novel. It is also related to the matter of historical investigation, a complex connection that is explored by Robin W. Winks in *The Historian as Detective*. In this anthology on aspects of the evaluation of evidence (with comments by the editor that point to parallels in crime fiction), various authors affirm "the strange nature of pure joy" in the discovery of truth, or even "the pleasures of doubt."[1] The historical paradigm has its literary counterpart. Why do we care if one or another fictive character killed an imaginary victim, or a victim who is irremediably dead, the murderer having also died long ago? The answer given by detective fiction is that is obviously matters *now,* since we and the detective and other characters are the ones who are presently engaged in the question. Even when it is totally oriented toward a past event, the detective novel reaffirms the process of its motion in time: forward or backward, in whatever segment of the process it is moving. The detective novel thus confirms another crucial concept in contemporary fiction: the acts of writing and reading are in themselves the substance of the book while it is being written or read.

This self-consciousness, which constantly equilibrates time, level of reality, and style, is a key to the form of the detective novel. To overlook this aspect of the detective novel leads to basic misunderstandings. Julian Symons, who has an obvious distaste for detection, thus misinterprets *The Daughter of Time* in *Mortal Consequences:*

> There is nothing new about this theory, as the student discovers at the end of their research, and Grant's almost total ignorance of history is the most remarkable thing about the book. The pleasure taken by critics in the very slow unfolding of a thesis already well known suggests a similar ignorance on their part. (p. 159)

This is a perfect way to miss the boat.

Tey's novel is not a piece of historical research, although it is ironically cast in that mold. It describes a full circle and returns to the beginning: one theory against another; this is part of its "message." Symons unwittingly states another part of the "message," "the pleasure taken by critics in the very slow unfolding of a thesis already well known." But then again — once more the balance is redressed — the thesis is not only a thesis; it deals with historical fact, which has deep roots and also branches reaching out into the future. A fact established by history can be taken to be real. Yet the questions posed by its interpretations and an evaluation of its consequences are comparable to those raised by imaginary events: possible analogies are persuasively presented in Winks's *The Historian as Detective*. History does not write itself; both the past and the future fully engage human responsibility.

3 The Detectives:
Methods, Methodology, and the Powers of Mind

The world of the detective novel is the world of man, bounded by the law on one side and criminal chaos on the other. Here man is at the same time the criminal and the judge. Albert Camus has shown the tragic paradox of the humanistic position in *La Chute:* the "judge-penitent" is one and the same person. Only the "author's intention," as Dorothy Sayers said, directs the action toward the morality of the end and gives it a conventional teleological aim. Once we have entered this structure, we find a cast of characters who are all potential suspects. There is only one major exception, the detective, whom we assume — whom we must assume — to be a trustworthy guide. The structural corollary is simply that we see very little of the mystery except through the eyes of this all-important character.

The detective is often the central consciousness, mostly a dramatic one, of the detective novel. His mind is the stage of the action; his activities give it form; his conclusion is the orchestration of the themes of the work. But sometimes there is a narrator, through whose perception we see the action. Also, there are often pairs of detectives, derived from the Holmes-Watson combination; one is major, the other minor. A police officer may be in charge of the investigation, but be helped by a private citizen who turns out to be the central figure, as is the case in Clinton-Baddeley, in Allingham, in Kemelman's novels, and in many others. The discussions between the two investigators may counterpoint methods or attitudes. The hierarchy may be reversed, when the police officer is the main investigator, assisted by somebody who provides his own thoughts or expertise on a subject.

The author may present quick scenes of action that are or are not clues to the mystery and of which the detective is unaware. In the novels by Maj Sjöwall and Per Wahlöö, episodes with supernumeraries (criminals, other policemen, or ordinary citizens) are interspersed with scenes presenting the main police officer. In *Unnatural Causes* by P. D. James, we see "the corpse without hands . . . in the bottom of a small sailing dinghy" (p. 7) before Superintendent Adam Dalgliesh arrives on the scene; we see glimpses of Oliver Latham suspiciously "stepping back . . . into the shadows of his upstairs room" (p. 18), and Alice Kerrison ominously thinking about "burying [someone?]" (p. 19). But these sidelights are only small openings in the construction. Some of the hints are red herrings, which will later be accounted for in the summary of the case. Some only bring air and light into the closed structure.

What seems more important is the relation between the detective's basic knowledge and our own. In the tradition of "fair play" that is prevalent in the detective story, the reader possesses all the information used by the detective. This rule, when observed, has often led to unseemly contortions on the author's part. Some apparently trivial detail, which the reader has inevitably forgotten, becomes a crucial lead, so that the Holmesian clues—from a small piece of string to the proverbial cigarette ash—become relevant. Agatha Christie sometimes succumbs to that temptation, although, more frequently, Hercule Poirot draws some connection or piece of evidence out of his hat at the important moment. There seems to be an awkwardness here, as if the author had a guilty conscience. The reason is that Hercule Poirot, especially in the earlier novels, is still the Holmesian embodiment of clear and logical reason, "the thing in the world most properly divided," in Descartes's philosophy. Sitting at home, Poirot can best solve the problem by using his "little gray cells." If he operates by the superior discipline of his pure and universal reason, he should know only what anyone else could know with the help of the same powers of concentration. (Is it possible that Poirot may also have a Nietzschean strain, as has been detected in S. S. Van Dine's Philo Vance?) When he then asks obscure questions with apparent irrelevance—what color were her eyes? What make were his boots?—Poirot is supposedly pursuing a line of thought that the reader should be pursuing too, were he only alert enough and sufficiently lucid.

But the author as well as her hero have moved away from these excessive constraints and have become more flexible and skeptical. In *Elephants Can Remember* (1972), for example, Poirot is mellower than he has ever been. In a long conversation with Chief Superintendent Garroway and Superintendent Spence (in Chapter 5), wisdom is equally divided between Garroway and Poirot, who speaks more of intuition and experience than of reason:

> One does come across these things sometimes. The proofs are there, the motive, the opportunity, the clues, the *mise-en-scène*, it's all there. . . . But all the same, those whose profession it is, *know*. They know that it's all wrong, just like a critic in the artistic world knows when a picture is all wrong. (p. 77)

The modified views of Poirot do not have altogether felicitous results. The plot becomes too obvious. This time we really do have more or less the same information as Poirot, and Poirot's point of view is not strong or stimulating enough to compensate for that.

This partial failure is instructive. It stems from the fact that Poirot (and Agatha Christie) straddle two conceptions: the plot-oriented one of the short story and the freer idea of the detective novel. In the latter, it does not matter whether the detective knows more than the reader. The notion that the detective should not know more comes from the puzzle theory in its rationalistic and mechanistic bias. In modern novels, the detective is often a "point of view" in the Jamesian sense. And he is always a character, with his own weaknesses and strengths. He looks at what he finds through his own tastes, limits, and professional habits. The reader is not, symbolically, a partner in a game with him, but follows his thought processes in a novel that is refracted mostly through the detective's mind. For purposes of suspense, therefore, the detective often does know more than we do. Sometimes he does not, and this too can produce special insights.

In *Death on the Agenda* by Patricia Moyes, the psychological point of view is used with effective irony in a case about which everyone (including the reader) knows as much, essentially, as everyone else. We share the perspective of Henry Tibbett, detective and accused. One guilty character turns out to be the girl with whom Tibbett had half fallen in love, who was presented in all her appealing integrity and straightforwardness. The thought may have crossed the reader's mind that she was the one who had the opportunity, but we reject the idea just as Tibbett does, because it seems unlikely. We have become deluded with him, and share his eventual discovery as well. What could be a trick is presented here with sophistication and plausibility, informed by the truth it reveals.

A police officer in a detective novel needs to redeem himself by some particularly endearing trait. Henry Tibbett is not only sensitive and kind but also humble and vulnerable. In Frances and Richard Lockridge's works, Inspector Merton Heimrich is touchingly clumsy and eager to please his perceptive and delicate wife. Their Lieutenant Shapiro seems to carry the sorrow of the world on his stooped shoulders and reads poetry besides. Josephine Tey's Inspector Grant is knowledgeable about the theater and appreciates poetry. P. D. James's Superintendent Dalgliesh even writes poetry. As for Sjöwall and Wahlöö, their Martin Beck is so sadly disappointed in his own family life that he becomes a symbol of modern middle-class depression. One of the most systematic redemptions of the profession may be in the figure of Dorothy Uhnak's Detective Christie Opara, a young policewoman whose husband, also a policeman, was killed in the line of duty.

The role of the police can present a delicate problem. Prejudice, literary tradition, and attitudes fostered by history past or present can produce distrust and hostility toward the police. Echoes of heroism in the figure of the detective set up the anticipation that he will rebel against the oppressive machinery and the brutal amoralism of the police force. This anticipation is less powerful in England than it is in the United States and especially in France, where, at least since the infamous heyday of spying under Napoleon III, the police can hardly elicit immediate approbation. It may be worth noting how primly Poirot sometimes insists that he is not French but Belgian. (Agatha Christie tells us in her *Autobiography* how her acquaintance with Belgian refugees during World War I suggested her retired police officer.) Is it by sheer coincidence that Simenon's Inspector Maigret of the Paris Police seems to reflect many values of his Belgian author?

In the United States, the novels of Rex Stout consistently show conflicts, as well as resolutions, between the police and Nero Wolfe (helped by Archie Goodwin). Here the question is fully explored, since some heroic, "hard-boiled" motifs in the detective's character meet the requirements of pure detection. Nero Wolfe, often called "the genius," is the almost caricatural embodiment of mind and reason, which work (albeit with notable exceptions) in a sedentary position. It is from his especially large armchair that Wolfe, in splendid isolation, solves cases in which the police, with all the equipment and staff at their disposal, have failed or erred. Archie Goodwin seems like Wolfe's active and brave counterpart, a detective of the American thriller tradition. Wolfe must be careful not to interfere with police procedure and certainly not to impede their investigation. Wolfe and Goodwin delight in defying Inspector Cramer and his Sergeant

Stebbins, and, although they cooperate, they also perversely insist on their legal rights. Inspector Cramer, red-faced, ill-mannered, and frequently chewing on his unlit cigar — when he tries to discard it he invariably misses the wastebasket in Wolfe's office — is nevertheless no fool. Whatever his angry bark and glacial eyes may suggest, he bows to justice, never blinded by his rage. We have no interest, of course, in Cramer's methods, which are only alluded to; our attention is directed to Wolfe's reasoning and morality as well as to Goodwin's resourcefulness.

The gentleman-amateur of Holmesian fame is still an active tradition, with solid symbolic foundations, in detective novels. In his role as "judge-penitent," or at least as investigator-penitent, the central figure is both inside and outside society. If the detective is totally immersed in his profession, his point of view can become too limited and specialized. Many novels start with a situation in which the police refuse to reopen a case (or look too far), so that the amateur must take it upon himself to follow his intuition. In *A New Lease of Death* (1967), Ruth Rendell shows fully how and why Chief Inspector Wexford, a competent and decent man, is psychologically incapable of developing a new view of an old case, partly from self-interest, partly from his unavoidable habits of thought, and partly because the evidence justifies him. Painfully and slowly, a clergyman, Archery, will have to take the initiative without the help of the police. Freedom of movement (Detective Opara is in danger of being demoted, not to speak of physical risks) and freedom of thought that brings fresh insight are the advantages of the amateur. The scope of the novel is expanded when the central consciousness of the investigator is not professionally committed to the action. This is as true of the novels of Henry James as it is of detective fiction.

A wide range of professions is represented by the amateurs: lawyers (more and more frequently), professors, clergymen, and financiers (in Emma Lathen). Retired ladies without a current profession, on the model of Miss Marple, still make interesting characters (in Elizabeth Lemarchand, for example). Writers (especially authors of detective novels, like Agatha Christie's Mrs. Oliver or Harriet Vane in Dorothy Sayers) can be helpful adjuncts. The methods of these detectives, derived from business, or literature, or law, applied to the situations they find, form a dynamic, coherent pattern.[1] The methodological influence can also work backward and be determined by the milieu in which the crime took place: medicine in Josephine Bell's *Double Doom* (1957) or P. D. James's *Shroud for a Nightingale* (1971); psychoanalysis in Amanda Cross's *Last Analysis;* the world of fashion in Margery Allingham's *The Fashion in Shrouds* (1938); and the theater in *False Scent* (1960) by Ngaio Marsh or Josephine Tey's *To Love and Be Wise* (1950). In those cases, professional consultants, as it were, usually help the police investigator.

Let us look at a relevant example, the workings of Rabbi Small's Talmudic mind. Let us catch the Rabbi on Sunday. (Now that Harry Kemelman has taken him through the days of the week, let us hope for an ingenious new time-space.) Sometimes it is the rabbi's reasoning that takes its inspiration from the Talmud, but on Sunday his method is geared to principles of morality. In *Sunday the Rabbi Stayed Home* we see the young, nearsighted, pale, and thin rabbi sheepishly going "through the service at breakneck speed" because he is going on a trip. Rabbi David Small is not a hero and not a saint, although he is more of both than the members of his congregation or of society in general. The themes of the novel turn around the discrimination between "normal" sins — cattiness, nastiness, selfishness, pride — and major ones. But what establishes these themes firmly in the world of detective fiction is that, according to the Rabbi, the result is what counts:

> "I don't understand you, David." Miriam pressed her fist against her mouth, as though to stifle harsh words of reproof. "He came to make amends. He was trying hard to effect a reconciliation. And he's a good man."

"Of course, he's a good man. And so are Gorfinkle and the rest of them. They're all good men, or they wouldn't be so concerned about what may happen to a poor Negro that stumbled into a mess of trouble. But goodness is not enough. The people who took part in the religious wars were good men, but they killed and maimed in the tens of thousands nevertheless."

"Oh, David, you're so—so inflexible. Can't you bend a little?"

He looked at her in surprise. "I bend when I have to, and I can. But I've got to be careful not to bend so far that I'll fall over." (p. 173)

Rabbi Small tells Lanigan, chief of the police force of Barnard's Crossing, a parable about the holiday of Passover, which "is associated with a specific commandment that is central in our law: 'And if a stranger sojourn with thee in your land, ye shall not do him wrong. . . .' " This is a moral commandment, which seems to have little to do with finding the criminal. Yet the Rabbi proposes it as a working hypothesis that will free the investigation from prejudice and falsehood. Lanigan says:

"The Jenkins Defense Committee [that has been formed] . . . will just be a lot of propaganda about social justice and the rights of the underprivileged and Lord knows what all. And it won't have any bearing on this case, because Jenkins is going to get a fair trial, and it's got nothing to do with whether he's black, white, or green with yellow polka dots."

"I'm not sure. Are you giving him a fair shake? It seems to me that you've made up your mind that he's guilty."

"I don't decide whether he's guilty or not. That's up to a judge and jury." (p. 177)

The point is that judgment is implicit in the way the crime is investigated. Everybody is responsible, just as man is responsible for himself and cannot blame God "for unpleasant and wicked things that happen" (p. 155). Lanigan cannot wash his hands of the judgment. He is not *the* judge or the jury, but he is also a judge or a jury. Rabbi Small explains:

> "But when he told his story, didn't you automatically assume those parts that indicated he was guilty were true and those that suggested he might be innocent a pack of lies?
>
> "You've always got to choose from the available material what you'll believe and what you won't. You know that." (p. 177)

Here again, evidence is not enough. It is the detective's particular commitment that filters reality and finally brings truth to light. Ideas are stated schematically here. The investigation is not so simple, as Rabbi Small and the police go on discussing evidence and theory, and the plot keeps shifting the patterns. But Rabbi Small is right, and his congregation will learn to see it. In spite of all his difficulties with them, Rabbi Small will get his sabbatical year off—an appropriate symbol. As God needed to rest, so does the rabbi need a rest from his congregation and the congregation from him.

A professional bent can also lead a detective astray, at least initially. Amanda Cross plays on this possibility in *The Question of Max* (1976). Her heroine-detective, Kate Fansler, professor of English literature with a specialty in Victorian fiction, bases her suspicion of murder on motives that are more congruent with a fanciful nineteenth-century character than present-day reality: a desire, on the murderer's part, to conceal his illegitimate birth and the fact that he was not related to a duke. This error, which almost costs Kate Fansler her life, is an interesting twist in amateur reasoning. It is unfortunately trivialized by being so flimsily founded from the start, and by being corrected so unconvincingly. The detective was only partly wrong in the motive, but right in the identity of the murderer. The novel never fully shows the reasons why, or the methods used to discover the truth at the end. Everyone, even Poirot, makes mistakes, sometimes catastrophic ones.

But when the detective is their author, only he can correct them. In detective fiction, the detective is the ultimate access to justice.

It would seem as if the model for the detective method, especially in contemporary works, should be historical — at least as a hypothetical pattern. Robin W. Winks's *The Historian as Detective* is so persuasive in showing the detective strain in historical evaluations that the temptation is strong to reverse the proposition and to say that, if the historian can be seen as a detective, the detective can also be seen as a historian. Winks rightly warns against this easy confusion. The detectives' obligations are not only to truth, and their functions in the novels do not allow for a full, scholarly search of past reality. Also, different professions and patterns of reasoning among detectives as well as consultants strongly inflect the investigation, for better (as in the case of Rabbi Small) or for worse. But if relativity in the view of truth is thus emphasized, the detective nevertheless leads to "a certain justice" and a certain justness of judgment that spring from a determination of what happened in the past.

4 The Detectives:
Eccentricity, Moral Truth, and the Creature Comforts

What do you think of Lord Peter Wimsey? This question may be as good as any to tell the men — or, at least as often, the women — from the boys, and to distinguish those who appreciate detective novels from those who do not. Dorothy Sayers's detective of the dropped final g's (as in "disappearin'") has probably been the target of more criticism than any other detective character: a rich, snobbish amateur, who pedantically looks at wine labels (in spite of his obvious ignorance of vintages and châteaux), and who, with intolerable smugness, solves mysteries through his monocle. "It would be charitable to think [writes Symons] that Wimsey . . . was conceived as a joke, but unhappily there is every indication that Sayers regarded him with the most tender feelings" (p. 109). Here we are again at the parting of the ways. Is Lord Peter a comic character? Of course he is, with his scrawny, cranelike neck, and his overstated un-derstatements — at least as comic as Dickens's Mr. Micawber.

George Grella sketches a comic mythology among classic detectives: the dandy, the elf, and the wizard — archetypes that subsume the varieties of detective heroes. Grella sees the detectives as stylized characters whose conception is more akin to comedy than to the novel or to detection: "There is more of Shakespeare, Congreve, and Sheridan than Poe, Conan Doyle, and Chesterton in their creation."[1] Ian Ousby also refers to a comic tradition: "In modern detective fiction the detective plays a role like that of the Duke in Shakespearean comedy: a moral hero and a figure of power, he establishes intellectual certainties and restores the order which has previously been threatened."[2] A comic presentation is often dominant in the initial portrait of the detectives.

Lord Peter is comic when he is comic — this truism reflects a novelistic truth. He is also utterly serious, and admirable, and poignantly lovable. In *Gaudy Night,* vestiges of mockery in Lord Peter turn almost entirely to self-mockery; he says to Harriet Vane:

> Old habits die hard. I will not promise to reform altogether. I shall, with your permission, continue to propose to you, at decently regulated intervals — as a birthday treat, and on Guy Fawkes Day and on the Anniversary of the King's Accession. But consider it, if you will, as a pure formality. You need not pay the smallest attention to it. (p. 55)

Here we see his irrepressible habit of observing obsolete rituals. But here also are evident his persistence, his understanding, and his humility.

Critics have blamed Dorothy Sayers for abandoning her earlier conception of the character, and, in *Gaudy Night,* for having "fallen in love" with Lord Peter. This is a naive way of seeing something that is essential in novel writing. Stendhal mellowed more and more toward a paternal affection for his heroes. Thomas Mann, during the composition of *Doctor Faustus,* explained that he was "falling in love" with his character. A loving perspective is an intrinsic part of a character. In *Gaudy Night,* the point of view that is sustained throughout is that of Harriet Vane, who is the central consciousness of the novel. This opens up the novel in several directions, which radiate from Harriet's role as well as her perception of the events. But in relation to Lord Peter, Harriet "rounds off" his character in an interesting way. If she detects a certain "stiffness" in his manner, it turns out that he has cracked two ribs in the course of his last case. If she continues rebuffing his proposals of marriage, it is no doubt for a number of reasons, the most powerful being that she owes Peter too much. Lord Peter has saved Harriet's life on a previous occasion, and it is hard to live on that level of noble heroism. They both have to play it down, just as Lord Peter continually plays himself down, until they reach the bantering balance of their relations and can finally agree to marry.

Lord Peter is mocking and mocked — all good detectives tend to be. There is a consistent irony in their presentation, but in variable doses. First, the detective is often an eccentric of the good old English school. He may be an old bachelor (like Hercule Poirot, who is also a foreigner, or Dr. Davie); or a middle-aged bachelor (Grant, Campion, Dalgliesh); a spinster (Miss Marple); or a widow (Mrs. Oliver, Elizabeth Lemarchand's Olivia Strode). Their detachment from the turbulence of daily life endows them with special perception. But many recent detectives lead their own family lives and are a part of the society in which they move. Here, too, Lord Peter has pioneered the way. (Agatha Christie seems to follow suit in *Postern of Fate*, which presents her couple of now elderly detectives.) Some detectives have marital difficulties. They may be divorced, like Martin Beck, or tragically widowed, like Detective Christie Opara (in contrast to older ladies like Mrs. Oliver, whose status seems to be permanent widowhood). Gideon in the works of J. J. Marric (also under the name of John Creasey) is a solid, likable pater familias, but his relations with his pianist daughter or his teenage son are sometimes complex and difficult; he is bound to his wife Kate by renewed affection and love, but only after a stormy estrangement.

Some detectives are handsome, like Alleyn, and some (like Maigret) are pot-bellied and stout. Some are lanky and red-haired (Lieutenant Shapiro), some are dowdy and round (Mrs. Oliver or Olivia Strode), and quite a few look conspicuously ordinary (Henry Tibbett or Merton Heimrich or Campion). In some cases, we do not really know. Many detectives are described by gesture, expression, and "allure" more than by physical characteristics, like Phoebe Atwood Taylor's Asey Mayo: "His mouth was wide, with a humorous twist about the corners, and his deep-set blue eyes twinkled disconcertingly. He usually walked with his shoulders hunched and his head thrust forward. An old broad-brimmed Stetson set at an angle on his head gave him a strangely rakish look" (*The Cape Cod Mystery*, p. 54). The portrait does not need to have the formulaic touches of Poirot's mustache or his patent leather shoes. But there is always a certain irony that punctures the heroic aspect and the structural authority of the detective. If nothing else, Henry and Emily Tibbett describe themselves as inalterably "dull."

Indeed the irony may be introduced by the detective himself and taken up again in different contexts. When Albert Campion looks in the mirror at himself and his sister Val (in *The Fashion in Shrouds*), the initial image is very apt in the world of dress designing where Val is a star:

> Campion put an arm round her shoulders and they stood for a moment admiring themselves with the bland self-consciousness of the nursery. "If I didn't look so half-witted we should be very much alike," he remarked presently. . . . "I think you're better than I in one or two ways, but I'm always glad to note that you have sufficient feminine weaknesses to make you thoroughly inferior on the whole." (pp. 6–7)

Campion's male chauvinism (itself partly self-conscious and ironic) is a theme that runs through this novel, in which women have a crucial role and highly developed intelligence in business and mechanics as well as in detection. And sometimes Campion is roundly taken to task for his narrow-minded views. Like all good detectives, he is ready to learn and mend his ways.

Not, perhaps, all his ways. This brings us to the heavy artillery that has been brought to bear on English detective novels of the 1920s and 1930s, the attacks against their "snobbish" values. Colin Watson, in *Snobbery with Violence,* hunts down snobbishness wherever he can find it in crime literature. Some of his examples are convincing, but detective fiction is a special case. To be sure, detectives tend to be aristocrats; even a professional policeman like Ngaio Marsh's Alleyn has a mother who is a *grande dame* of high society. And Campion, self-deprecating and sensitive though he may be, makes abundant fun of his valet Mr. Lugg, whose cockney accent and defective manners often unnerve him. Campion has saved Lugg from a life of crime, and he likes and respects his valet. But that may only reinforce the condescension that is inherent in Campion's attitude.

Snobbishness of a kind, although not necessarily super-ciliousness, is a crucial element in the morality of detective fiction. We return to this question in Chapter 5, but the luxuries enjoyed by Lord Peter or Campion and others are not marks of snobbishness. Julian Symons finds unforgivable such sentences spoken by Lord Peter Wimsey's valet Bunter on the first page of *Clouds of Witness* by Dorothy Sayers: " 'Good morning, my lord. Fine morning, my lord. Your lordship's bath-water is ready.' " This is certainly not a masterpiece of lively dialogue, but as Dr. Davie says, "what's the matter with it" — considering, especially, its ironic function? Lord Peter is genuinely a wealthy member of the nobility, for whom it is perfectly natural to have his bath drawn in the morning; it is not snobbish of him to do this or to have his valet announce it. The utter comfort of this cozy tableau, however, will present an ironic contrast to the upheavals brought about by detec-tion. This is the key.

In presenting English society of the 1930s, it was reasonable for authors to select the aristocracy (or the near-aristocracy) as the milieu in which luxury, idleness, refinements of manners, taste, and gastronomy were the comforts of life. At the end of *The Fashion in Shrouds,* when Campion and Amanda decide to marry, comfort is the final note: "Do you know, Amanda, I'm not sure that 'Comfort' isn't your middle name." But they have earned it. The criminal, on the contrary, is an amoral follower of his comfort:

> The old superintendent was buttoning himself into his coat as he spoke. It was nearly dawn and there was a cold mist over the water meadows. "He's got exalted ideas of his own importance. A lot of them have. It's the commonest type of what you might call the 'elaborate' killer. I've seen it before. George Joseph Smith was one of them. They honestly think a bit of their cash or a bit of their convenience is worth someone else's life." (p. 254)

There lies the main moral difference between the criminal and the detective, who lets himself be persuaded by duty, at the risk sometimes of life and limb, when a human life is at stake, but often quite reluctantly. The detective is emphatically not a saint, monk, or superman, and he rarely seeks out a case. More often, it is forced on him by friends or by circumstance.

A vein of hedonism runs through the family portraits of detectives. Meals are important rituals, which pleasantly punctuate time, especially an English tea. "The science of Life (a Cambridge hedonist has proclaimed) depends on the placing of tea as near as possible to the ceremony of luncheon." This declaration of principle, from *My Foe Outstretch'd Beneath the Tree,* seems strangely reminiscent of the first sentence of Henry James's *Portrait of a Lady:* "Under certain circumstances there are few hours in life more agreeable than the hour dedicated to the ceremony known as afternoon tea." Perhaps the allusion in Clinton-Baddeley includes, intertextually, the whole opening paragraph of James, with its lyrical evocation of "the perfect middle of a splendid summer afternoon" and its suspension of time: "From five o'clock to eight is on certain occasions a little eternity."

The composition of menus is also important. Gastronomical descriptions abound, and Dr. Davie goes so far as to send someone the "authentic" recipe for *crème brûlée,* which figures as an appendix to the novel. The enormous bulk of Rex Stout's Nero Wolfe is an eloquent sign of *his* devotion, and the opulent recipes by Wolfe's cook Fritz have been published in a separate volume. Hercule Poirot can tell a good trout when he tastes one, and his portly figure attests to having partaken of a few such delights. The aroma of Madame Maigret's succulent *pot-au-feu* pursues Maigret (and the reader) as he makes his calls in various places, including bars where he regales himself with one "petit verre" after the other. Maigret presents a full, petit bourgeois, continental counterpart to the comfort-loving English aristocrats. Shod in slippers, Maigret likes to sit in front of his window, smoking his pipe and daydreaming. He likes quiet evenings and walks with his wife along the boulevards of Paris, and he plays cards with friends.

Other detectives may be more ambivalent or less consistent, but they do have a tendency to appreciate creature comforts. Some, who are less fortunately endowed than Maigret, find their ordinary life rather restricted and welcome special opportunities. Henry Tibbett is glad to go to Geneva for a convention in *Death on the Agenda,* and his wife Emily uses her household savings to accompany him there. And when an arrogant hostess in Geneva invites her out for lunch, Emily Tibbett savors the excellent wine and the chicken dish even though she feels somewhat slighted by the high-handedness of the rich woman. In *Cyanide with Compliments* by Elizabeth Lemarchand, Olivia Strode, a widow who has worked quite hard in her life, intensely enjoys every moment of her holiday, from the first sensations of flying to Venice to the sightseeing at various ports of call during the cruise. In her cabin, she relaxes in luxurious ease:

Her bed was certainly very comfortable when she eventually reached it. She lay propped up against her pillows, book in hand and pervaded by a sense of well-being. . . . Looking ahead, the prospect of a lazy day at sea on the morrow was attractive. Further ahead still was the excitement of seeing at last places which she had longed to visit: Athens, for instance, and Troy and Cnossos. (p. 10)

Symbolically, these middle-class, or lower middle-class, or upper-class pleasures are the detective's right. They constitute the normal life, which it is his mission to preserve. Paradoxically, to preserve it the detective must leave his everyday existence abruptly, often not knowing whether he will be able to return to it. That is his risk and his glory. After he has rid the world of "the pest," in Poirot's phrase, thereby making this normal life available to others, he can savor his drink on his sunny terrace, like Inspector Heimrich, or even play very bad chess with a friend, like the melancholy Swede, Martin Beck — until the next case comes along.

5 A Language for the Happy Few: Authenticity and Symptomatic Meanings

Lord Peter may drop his g's and sometimes speak like a comic-book gentleman, and Hercule Poirot uses his unlikely gallicisms (which tended to drop out of his speech as the years went on). Asey Mayo—"the kind of man everybody expects to find on Cape Cod and never does"—has a strange parlance of his own, a combination of chewing tobacco and "his trick of pronouncing no more syllables of a word than were absolutely necessary" (*The Cape Cod Mystery,* p. 44). But these are mannerisms, comparable to the rakish slant of a hat or a monocle that may only be a magnifying glass in disguise. What matters is what these characters are saying through their disguises.

Asey Mayo observes: "Restaurants call fried flounder filly of sole, but it's flounder. They's more'n one man in this world who's travelin' under a different name" (p. 55). And Dr. Davie in *My Foe Outstretch'd Beneath the Tree* thinks:

No one up to 1930 had ever treated "How d'you do?" as a question requiring an answer, or rather the correct answer was to say "How d'you do" back again. But nowadays people seemed to think they ought to supply a bulletin. He knew how it had happened: the words that used to be murmured with formality were nowadays screamed and italicized. "My dear! How *are* you?" was the way they did it now, and it is very difficult to say "How d'you do?" in reply to that. Davie usually said "In a rapid decline" or "Not

39

much better," which was apt to fling the stranger off balance. (p. 11)

Although their ideas may seem contradictory, Asey Mayo and Dr. Davie are really saying the same thing. They are both speaking about language, which has denotative meanings and connotative ones; it has a grammar set down by rules, but also a network of usage. There are dialects and there are idiosyncrasies of speech, which may or may not be understood by some. Asey Mayo knows all about fish (as well as most other things), and he knows that it is still the same whether you call it by one name or another. But when restaurants say "filly of sole," they are not mistaken about the real thing. They have a purpose: to delude the tourist, who prefers an elegant sole to a local flounder. If a criminal changes his name, he also has a purpose. In a complementary way, when "How are you?" is "screamed and italicized," it has a literal meaning that is far removed from its purpose as a perfunctory greeting. But the literal meaning is false—witness the reaction. If you really inform the questioner about your state of health or general well-being, it will indeed "fling him off balance."

There are conventions in language as in bridge. In *My Foe Outstretch'd Beneath the Tree:*

> "You play bridge," said Davie, "and I don't understand that. Forty years ago, in the days of auction, I played quite a bit—but I never learnt the new rules. One must not, I believe, kick one's partner under the table or pass him a note, but there seems to be a sort of code whereby you convey the information nevertheless. One says three diamonds over two clubs and one's partner immediately divines by preconcerted plan that one has the ace of hearts." (p. 86)

Conventions can function as signals, like kicks under the table, or winks that establish complicity between characters or between certain characters and the reader. Detective fiction itself may be a convention of this kind.

But people who are steeped in their own usages may not be aware of their provincialism (which can be turned against them). An amusing detail in *Gaudy Night* shows how Harriet found a viable pretext for staying at Oxford:

> It was a matter of mild public interest at Shrewsbury College that Miss Harriet Vane, the well-known detective novelist, was spending a couple of weeks in College, while engaged in research at the Bodleian upon the life and works of Sheridan Le Fanu. The excuse was good enough; Harriet really was gathering material, in a leisurely way, for a study of Le Fanu, though the Bodleian was not, perhaps, the ideal source for it. But there must be some reason given for her presence, and Oxford is willing enough to believe that the Bodleian is the hub of the scholar's universe. (p. 107)

The magic words do their trick — "engaged in research . . . upon the life and works" open up the gates of the self-satisfied illusions of Oxford. A little seasoning is added: "Well-known detective novelist," and all is well in this perfect world. A lack of self-consciousness and self-awareness turns the users of conventions into easy preys or objects of ridicule. We have already seen in Chapter 1 how the style of Maurice Seton, in *Unnatural Causes,* is used for purposes of parody. The style of the other suspects in that novel is equally comic.

Written or spoken style is a crucial element in the portrait of many characters of detective fiction. It recurs almost everywhere in more or less extended examples. In *A Serious Investigation* by Lesley Egan, an important suspect, Palatine, is a writer of popular books about spiritualism. Jesse, the lawyer and detective of the novel, describes Palatine to his friend (and future brother-in-law) Andrew Clock, the police sergeant who looks like a "dumb cop," with his Neanderthal jaw and his professional bluntness, but is shrewd and compassionate:

> "I've read a couple of his books. Mr. Palatine's a smart-aleck, Andrew. You know, or maybe you don't, that there's

a lot of activity going on in the field of parapsychology—
newest name for it—right now. . . . Palatine's just cashing
in on it. Getting in on the act. With the popular books,
written all light and entertaining for the lay reader. Way I
read him. Way he comes through in his prose style, you get
me, he doesn't believe in any of it." (p. 33)

Later, Mr. De Witt, the director of the Institute of
Parapsychology, a correct and scholarly-looking character,
concurs in his own view (and style) about Palatine: "Yes indeed. He pretends it *is* his subject, but actually all the
nuances—if one can find nuances in light prose—downgrade
the entire subject, all the really serious investigation" (p. 63).
And here is Palatine himself speaking:

"I had been slightly more interested than usual at the sitting
that evening—what purported to be some cross-cor-
respondence. Of course, terribly monotonous and passé,
claiming to emanate from A. Conan Doyle, but. . . ."
(p. 35)

Palatine's affectations are not only reflected in his speech but
also in his too youthful navy blazer, his toupee, his ruby and
gold ring, the crème de menthe he sips from a tiny glass, and
the furniture of his expensive apartment.

Language is more than mere words. Style pervades
everything, and here we enter a vast area of detective fiction,
in which gesture, clothes, furniture, mannerisms of all kinds,
hobbies, and tastes are clues to character. This is exactly the
neoclassical "moral" perspective. La Bruyère, a seventeenth-
century critic of French society, stated it eloquently: "A fool
neither talks, nor walks, nor sits down like a man of wit." But
La Bruyère, who was often harshly satirical, had a fairly clear
idea of what a man of wit was. This has become, however, a
complex question. "Fashion and Tradition are continually at
war, and Fashion always wins. Resist Fashion and you're an
old fuddy duddy," says Dr. Davie (p. 13). Harriet Vane does

not begrudge some people (like Mr. Jenkyn) their little amusements with fashion, "being old enough to know that even the most crashing social bricks make but a small ripple in the ocean of time, which quickly dies away" (*Gaudy Night,* p. 207).

There is fashion and fashion. What, for example, is the meaning of a word like "camp"? As seen in *My Foe Outstretch'd Beneath the Tree:*

> "I wouldn't bother to find out," said Davie. "The word had a meaning twenty years ago. For a coterie it had an exact and entertaining meaning (though from what derived, Lord knows). Then it was taken up by the gigglers and the despoilers, who used it for everything. Today the word means nothing at all. It's been run to death and can't ever be revived. . . ."
>
> "But what *was* the original meaning of 'camp,' Dr. Davie?" said Miss Cragg.
>
> "Well—let me see. A calculated extravagance, a kind of archness, a scarcely perceptible wink, a public display of a private understanding—oh, a sort of secret masonic saucebox."
>
> "It sounds like a poem by Gerard Manley Hopkins," said Miss Eggar. "And I don't think it is at all a fair description of the dining-room curtains." (p. 14)

Even in fashion, the word can fit the thing. "Camp" does not seem to fit the curtains at all, just as a violin stand is not good for lecturing; Davie prefers a lectern. "One needs to be very short to be able to make use of that [a violin stand]. And they collapse at dramatic moments."

Whether there are fashions in crime and motivations is a question that recurs in different contexts. It is bandied about by Val and Campion toward the beginning of *The Fashion in Shrouds.* Val says to her brother:

> "You're *vieux jeu,* my pet. . . . Like most men you're between three and five years out of date. Don't you notice a

change in the fashion?. . . . Today anything can happen. People can wear *anything*, say *anything*, do *anything*."

Much later, she sums up the argument:

"I do have to explain things in detail to you. I thought you were so hot on understanding people."
"I've been cheating all these years. I'm really Alice in Wonderland," said Mr. Campion humbly. "Still, I'm picking up a crumb or two now in my fiddling little way." (p. 59)

The detective has to learn to understand (if not necessarily to speak) several languages, according to the people among whom he is investigating. This is particularly true of policemen and professional detectives, but even an amateur like Lord Peter Wimsey knows how to appear charming — to everyone's surprise — in the proper milieu of Shrewsbury College. And Campion has to pick up a crumb or two of a different language as well.

But the detective has his own language, as other characters do. There is a close understanding among certain characters (usually, but not always, including the detective) who speak the same language. Detectives often react with immediate antipathy to people who offend their taste. In *A Serious Investigation,* Jesse visits Anita Rooper, a suspect:

The girl was a cheap girl, you could read that: no background, Margaret Brandon had put it. There hadn't been an ounce of snobbery in her and it wasn't that the girl was from a poor family or anything like that. But people did forever come all shapes and sizes, and the girl was cheap, probably amoral, all-on-the-surface female. . . . She was chewing gum. She was a blonde by request and she needed a touch-up rinse. (p. 20)

These are obvious principles of discrimination at work. The dissolute-looking, gum-chewing, bleached blonde is a commonplace that is often evoked (in Ross Macdonald among others). But taste may be more esoteric, or simply eccentric sometimes. Hercule Poirot is tolerant enough to know that most of his visitors shudder at the thought of drinking one of his "sirops," and considerate enough, when Mrs. Oliver comes to see him, to have a drink prepared that *she* may like: a strong coffee or a liqueur.

Tastes may be more or less significant, more or less arbitrary, and more or less symbolic, as in *My Foe Outstretch'd Beneath the Tree:*

> Davie had many pet dislikes: the plucked eyebrow, the painted cupid's bow which fails to conceal the thin cruel lip of a rapacious strumpet, the dark parting which betrays the truth about a head of golden hair. That especially gave him the willies. (p. 16)

Here again we are close to symptomatic meanings. And it is generally true that the detectives may indulge their eccentricities, their *gourmandise,* their love of one lore or another, but a *basso continuo* runs through most of their dislikes: they detest anything bogus. They despise the pretentious, the artificial, the ungenuine, whether it is bleached hair, painted toenails, toupees, calling flounder sole, feigning interest where there is none (as in "How *are* you?"), feigning knowledge, feigning compassion, and feigning altruism. They dislike busybodies with the wrong motives, fusspots unaware of the inconvenience they cause. "Why doesn't someone chuck her overboard?" asks Professor Charles Moreton-Blake about the fussy woman who threatens to become "the cruise menace, buttonholing the unsuspecting to tell them her life history, and gatecrashing other people's conversations" (*Cyanide with Compliments,* pp. 8-9). Olivia Strode is too kind to agree overtly, but we are sure of her understanding. Self-pitying characters, who conceal an inferiority complex under an egotism that is itself concealed, are favorite targets. The inauthentic is unmasked in all sorts of fields: in fishing, skiing, and medicine; in nursing and in banking; in the hotel business and in the Church; in mountain climbing, police work, and fashion designing; in academia— and even in crime.

In the area of tastes, discriminations become particularly important. This brings us back to the theme of labels and red-brick universities. Labels and prejudices fare badly in detective novels. Some rather general prejudice may be brought to light and examined carefully. In *A Serious Investigation,* for example, many conversations deal with the distinction between vulgar or hysterical spiritualism and serious interest in parapsychology. The victim was a particularly decent and honest medium (although the crime turned out to have no connection with this question). Jesse has read some books on the subject, in which he seems rather interested, but Palatine, who grossly "cashes in" on the public's ignorance and unholy fascination, is nothing but a reprehensible psychopath.

Not surprisingly, detective novels are a favorite symbol, almost a conventional wink. Many detectives like to read them for relaxation and occasionally for information. Writers of detective fiction often have a part in the novel. Sometimes, thorough distinctions are made, such as between the pretentious nonsense written by Maurice Seton in *Unnatural Causes* and, implicitly, the book we are reading. In other words, the label of "mystery writer" means nothing. "It depends . . . on the brick." What is in a name is what it designates in a particular case. Flounder and sole may be quite different; if you like the one, the name of the other will not change it. Harriet Vane is such a full-fledged character that she needs no apology for her professional detective writing: she is completely and perceptively what she is. Mrs. Oliver, for instance, takes a different stand and seems to be quite modest about her writing, which is more for entertainment than for anything else.

The detectives tend to know what they like and whom they like. Although an immediate liking, an appeal, a charm, sometimes may play a part, it usually is a question of speaking a certain language and sharing a certain tone. Jesse and Nell, in the novels of Lesley Egan, present a schematic example. In their conversations, Nell often answers her husband's thought rather than his words, and Jesse marvels at this repeated phenomenon. Madame Maigret knows exactly when to let the inspector eat his dinner quietly without disturbing him with importunate questions, but she also knows how to be interested and to listen to his worries. She even knows how not to mind when her husband does not seem to notice what he is eating — a grave symptom in his case. In Sara Woods, Antony Maitland, tired as he may be of a week of "makeshift meals" (in *Though I Know She Lies*), understands why his wife Jenny, in this depressing November weather, must paint the kitchen again, using a jarring cerise color for the chairs. Olivia Strode, in *Cyanide with Compliments,* shares companionable small talk and even more companionable silences with her former employer, the history professor, and his wife. A husband-detective may listen to his Bach records while his wife "curls up" with a book by Charlotte Armstrong (in Lesley Egan). Father and son (in Michael Gilbert), uncle and nephew (in Sara Woods), husband and wife (in innumerable novels), and professional friends or colleagues, may understand each others' ways of going about a case and interpreting motivations.

Sometimes, it is not so much a professional point of view that is crucial, but an atmosphere of ease and familiarity. In *Unnatural Causes* by P. D. James, Dalgliesh comes to spend a ten-day holiday with his spinster aunt, Jane Dalgliesh, a rather austere, laconic woman, whom it is not easy to like:

> He suspected that Jane Dalgliesh thought it odd that an intelligent man should choose to earn his living catching murderers and she was not a woman to feign polite interest

when she felt none. She made no demands on him, not even the demands of affection, and because of this she was the only woman in the world with whom he was completely at peace. He knew exactly what the holiday offered. They would walk together, often in silence, on the damp strip of firm sand between the sea's foam and the pebbled rises of the beach. He would carry her sketching paraphernalia, she would stride a little ahead. . . . (p. 14)

Jane Dalgliesh presents the unity and integrity of an Indian sculpture (and its angularity as well), with her "long face, brown and carved as an Aztec's, the eyes hooded, the nose long and straight above a wide mobile mouth" (p. 20). She leads her routine-filled, quiet life with idiosyncratic dignity. If she is friendly with a famous writer, it is not because she has snobbish longings (unlike the other suspects in the novel), but because she has a long-established acquaintance with the writer and likes both him and his wife. She starts out on her habitual walk before her guest gets up in the morning, leaving him to get his own breakfast, and they both appreciate this mutual respect for each other's habits and likes.

What does all this indicate? Is there a moral grammar for this language of tastes? P. D. James poses the problem acutely. In *Unnatural Causes,* the likable and appealing characters (as well as others) still turn out to be innocent. But in *Shroud for a Nightingale* (1971), the author pursues the question. In this novel, very full character presentations — of the nurses and the doctors — turn around the themes of integrity, professionalism, and honesty. And the final irony is unrelieved: the criminal was a woman after Dalgliesh's own heart, or at least it seemed so. Dalgliesh intensely enjoyed his interviews with the matron, and appreciated her peaceful self-possession, her professional conscientiousness, her fairness to her students, her intelligence, and her understanding. There is no trick played here. The matron turns out not to be an excusable and understandable criminal, but a horrible one.

Dalgliesh — and the novel — again have to pull up short, and again, the balance must be redressed. The detective may bend, but, as Rabbi Small says, "not so far that [he'll] fall over." Taste, too, no matter how sound, can be a dangerous temptation and a delusion. The theme is clearly stated toward the beginning of *Shroud for a Nightingale* in a dialogue between Dalgliesh and Sergeant Masterson, who,

> most of the time, and for reasons which it seemed to him unprofitable to explore, . . . disliked him [Dalgliesh] heartily. He suspected that the antipathy was mutual, but this didn't particularly worry him. (p. 66)

The reasons for this antipathy have something to do with language, both literal and symbolic. When Dalgliesh asks his subordinates for information, it means that he

> now expected to hear a brief, succinct, accurate, elegantly phrased but comprehensive account of the crime. . . . Dalgliesh's subordinates were apt to complain that they hadn't realized that a degree in English was the new qualification for joining the C. I. D. (p. 65)

But Masterson, an ambitious and rather shallow young man, is saved by his very vanity, and he does his job. "Dalgliesh wasn't a man to prejudice a subordinate's career because he disliked him"; Masterson knows this.

"It has taken me a long time to learn my lesson, Harriet," says Lord Peter in the last pages of *Gaudy Night*. "I have had to pull down, brick by brick, the barriers I had built up by my own selfishness and folly." And after "the last kick that sent [his] vanity out of doors," he can set Harriet free, give her the freedom that was "hers already," and thus free himself too. Those are the delicate balances of morality, in which each character plays his part, as do musical phrases in the *Concerto in D Minor* played by the two violinists:

Peter, she felt sure, could hear the whole intricate pattern, every part separately and simultaneously, each independent and equal, separate but inseparable, moving over and under and through, ravishing heart and mind together.

Not all detectives are as fortunate as Lord Peter. Some emerge with empty hands after they have had to discard their tastes and their pride. But in these games of judgment and penitence, the penitent finally remains the judge in his essential humanity and morality. And the reader watches him, just as in *Gaudy Night* Harriet's

eyes were on one slight figure that crossed the cobbled square, walking lightly under the shadow of St. Mary's into the High. All the kingdoms of the world and the glory of them. (p. 381)

6 Why Murder?

Neither taste nor reason can prevent crime. By definition, in detective fiction nothing but the most inelegantly expeditious measures, such as catching the criminal, can prevent crime. This reality principle is firmly anchored in the structure, of which murder is the symbolic support. As in the existentialist perspective, the *given* is there; the novel does not move dramatically toward psychological and moral developments that produce and explain it. What, then, is the psychological and moral function of murder?

In his fascinating study of the "mythology" of the *roman policier*, Francis Lacassin analyzes the methods used by G. K. Chesterton's Father Brown, as well as the philosophical concerns of this priest-detective-philosopher. Lacassin shows that for Father Brown the main problem, contrary to the tradition of Sherlock Holmes, is not to discover who committed the crime, but how it was committed. Simenon's Maigret, equally patient and tepid in his search for the identity of the criminal, seems to concentrate on the "why." In both cases, the solution tends to produce an understanding that is colored by charity and tolerance: "human" on Maigret's side, Christian and godly on Father Brown's.[1]

There are crime novels in which the psychology of murder is central. William Irish, whose works have been used with excellent effect in film—*Rear Window, The Bride Wore Black,* and *Waltz into Darkness* in its French translation as *La Sirène du Mississippi*—specializes in a haunting use of point of

view in which the crime is seen subjectively. But these
explorations are tangential to detective fiction. There,
whodunit? is the working proposition throughout, and the
form the search takes offers various constellations around the
crucial question. The demands of the genre work together
with its underlying meanings, and all flirtations with
sympathy, justification, and indignation provoked by human
cruelty and social injustice must retain a largely "play"
character, because they must eventually bow to the realities of
law and a morality that is often complex and sophisticated but
ultimately conventional.

Detective novels generally undermine the myth of the heroic
criminal; most often there is nothing at all interesting in the
criminal's makeup or his motivation. Although tempting
notions may surface in the course of the investigation, the true
answer is usually drab and unsavory. One symptom of this
tendency is a conventional pattern that is sometimes observed:
the murderer may turn out to be one of the least significant
and least suspect characters who were presented from the
beginning; or, as a corollary, the *most* suspect and least
significant character. Rex Stout plays teasingly on this double
convention in *Please Pass the Guilt* (1972). Nero Wolfe and
Archie Goodwin are launched on this case by the sudden
appearance of a disturbed man who suffers from the Lady
Macbeth hallucination of blood on his hands. Unlikely as it
may seem, this minor character is so faintly present in the
course of the investigation that his ultimate guilt comes as a
surprise, but a logically satisfying one. The circle closes in
perfect plausibility, although the intricate inquiry seems to
lead away from the initial suspense at most points.
Psychological deduction, elements of construction, and moral
meaning all come together in this simple formula, by which
the immediate evidence is vindicated in complex, incompatible, and ironic ways.

The reason for the murder in *Please Pass the Guilt* could not
possibly be guessed at first. It could only be uncovered by the

painstaking efforts of the master detective and his equally masterful adjunct, and, as usual, by a good amount of luck. Many contemporary writers go further into the psychology of the murderer, although this is a game that is hard to play and even harder to win. Poirot often succeeds by sleight of hand, because his superior logic seems to make him invulnerable to terror and pity. But this cannot be taken too seriously; by fictional criteria, it is not legitimate. Insights into the murder's mind often border on terror when they occur in the course of the action and people's lives are in danger.

In *Take My Life,* Winston Graham presents a terrifying scene on a train. Philippa Shelley, the opera singer, who had set out to prove her husband's innocence of the murder of his former mistress, finds herself returning in the same compartment as the murderer, who expresses criminal as well as moral ideas in a long and imposing dialogue. The immediate danger that Philippa is in more than mitigates our interest in Fleming's distorted "virtue," and the novel returns to Philippa's thoughts on the ambiguity of the problem. Recollecting some of the murderer's words and phrases, Philippa thinks:

> "Gone Lovell's, gone Penmair, gone Fleming. I was a *good* man. I can take a dull boy and give him the glow of a new ambition. Moral values. All things were strong and rigid in him. To the last unbending. That was why Elizabeth [the victim] had gone, why she had not. Good and evil, born in one man, grown in one man, ruined together. . . ." (p. 189)

How far can the author go without, as Rabbi Small says, falling over? Detective fiction does not fall over. In *Take My Life,* no matter how pathetic Fleming's flaw, he has killed and is actively threatening two more lives (Philippa's and her accused husband's), about which we care much more than about the state of the murderer's soul.

Like tragedy, detective fiction avoids the presentation of monsters. If the rules of the detective story ban professional

crime and madness, it is because professional criminals and
lunatics are so obvious as suspects that they detract from the
interest of the plot. Their presence would obscure the question
of motive, which, in one way or another, remains essential.
Are there motives? Are there always motives or are there
crimes without motives? What is a motive? One has the
impression that some authors would like to put these questions
aside in order to develop their outlook on social realities. But
these questions seem irrepressible, especially in novels that put
the police investigation in the foreground and often offer long
discussions of motive. One rather common position taken by
contemporary police investigators is that it is not necessary to
establish motive in order to establish guilt, but it helps in the
search. But then the other side of the coin immediately
appears: What is a motive for murder? What is a possible
motive in contrast to a real one? Can anybody be a murderer,
given a sufficient motive? Or do criminals only need slight
motives? The answers vary considerably, but in all novels the
solution must strike a balance and combine clues and
reasoning that are derived from external factors with a more
or less explicit interpretation of motive.

Once a police investigation starts, the movement of the
novel is toward more widespread suspicion that is cast on more
and more characters. Members of the police are generally free
to interrogate whom they wish, so that the number of suspects
increases rapidly. Also, the police often claim to work without
preconceptions, so that their net is cast wide. Routine requires
some automatic suspicions: the husband or wife of the victim,
beneficiaries of wills, and the like. Private citizens playing the
role of detectives tend to work more selectively, through
circumstance and lack of means, but also by intellectual
inclination. Their patterns of thought must then shift to allow
for new discoveries or accommodate new evidence, whereas
the police, starting with a large mass of evidence, tend to
narrow their search as they go along. In both cases, the
widening of the circle of suspects reaches a high point toward

the middle of the action, after which the movement is stabilized or decreased.

Typically, the first movement reveals hidden facts in many suspects' lives, or at least errors and lies in their testimonies. Besides providing red herrings, these hidden facts may also have other meanings in different cases and contexts. To put it succinctly, "You start digging and you find things," as Sergeant Schroeder says in *Tuesday the Rabbi Saw Red* by Harry Kemelman (p. 171). One main effect of these little discoveries is to generalize the possibilities of guilt. Does this mean that everybody could be guilty?

The related questions are difficult to answer. They are fully and intelligently explored in Robert Bernard's *Deadly Meeting,* in which the setting is academic, and the action takes place among the faculty of a college. Bill Stratton, professor of English and chairman of his department, is put, through the murder, in the double position of colleague and detective helping the police. His acquaintance with the other members of the department propels him into reflections and emotions that always circle back to the same conclusion: it is inconceivable that any of these persons could be a murderer:

> He had told Moynahan [the police detective] that he knew them all too well to believe that one of them was a murderer. Perhaps he had been wrong. (p. 92)

Later on, as the number of suspects is narrowed down to four, Stratton still encounters the same obstacle:

> Moynahan nodded. "You're probably right about his innocence. That leaves four other men. In your frank opinion, which of them is the most apt to commit murder?"
> "I can't answer that question better than I could in Devonport. None of them seems like a murderer to me."
> "Fair enough. . . ." (p. 107)

The first paradox is that nobody seems like a murderer, yet somebody obviously is. Theoretically, therefore, anybody and everybody is a possible murderer. Only the discovery of the real murderer will cut the Gordian knot.

As the search progresses and more hidden facts appear in more people's lives, the problem is reversed with the same result: everybody seems suspect, therefore everybody is possibly guilty. (This is a schematic simplification that is much qualified by the psychological and moral shadings of the work.) At this step in the reasoning one may ask: Does this paradox mean that everybody could be a murderer? I believe not. Here again, the answer lies not in any statements made at one time or another in the novel but in the whole structure. *Deadly Meeting* throws light on the conditions that are inherent in the point of view, which define the truth at any given moment:

> Bill grimaced. It was never pleasant to know too much about another person. What he had been finding out about Peter made him realize how little he really knew of his colleagues. How many of them did he really understand? It was improbable that beneath the smooth surface of their routine, academic lives there was as much seething as there had been beneath Peter's exterior, but he could no longer feel sure. (p. 92)

The observer's view is limited and, to some extent, will remain so.

It is from within these limitations, however, that the truth must be found — which brings to the fore again the matter of motive. If *How?*, *Why?*, and *Who?* are the three questions that need answers, the detective of classical persuasion aims for the *Who?*, which functions as a reality principle behind the other questions. Ultimately, and for purposes of private meditation, some detectives are more interested in the why or the how; philosophic inquiry seeks reasons, whereas the more technical-minded concentrate on the ways and means.

Whatever their personal concerns, detectives in full-fledged modern novels, in which point of view is an essential element of structure, find that, in order to ferret out the criminal, they must in some way be able to understand the crime, not necessarily in all its psychological, moral, philosophical, religious, and social meanings, but enough to be able to point to its perpetrator. Again, a balance must be struck. The old controversy opposed Father Brown's desire to understand the criminal and the Holmesian search for external facts. As Lacassin shows, Father Brown's *How?* only leads to the further *Why?*, which is what really concerns Father Brown who tries to empathize with the criminal to the point of becoming (in thought) a criminal himself. And Father Brown explains that if he finds a crime horrible, it is not because he is not capable of committing it, but because he is (*Mythologie du roman policier,* p. 226). The complex manipulation of points of view in modern fiction no longer reflects reality in this clearly set-out pattern. Understanding entails a measure of empathy — although even sympathy is enough — but different approaches are possible and necessary: there are degrees of comprehension. Neither the author nor the detective can be omniscient; we must be satisfied with fragmentary results. Meetings of points of view, combinations of reality and possibility, and all structures of knowledge inform partial truths.

There can, however, be no discovery in detective novels without understanding. Although some detective novels flirt with the idea of crime without motive, the solution of the crime always shows one. What kinds of motives are prevalent? We have seen how Margery Allingham plays on the notion of fads in crime in *The Fashion in Shrouds.* Other novels deal with a wide range of possible motives. Works presenting a well-defined milieu — hospitals, psychoanalytic practice, the church, Wall Street, fashion, the university, law — usually bring up the question of how diverse and how special motives can be. Given the intricacies of the medical hierarchy in a hospital, could a physician murder for professional ambition? Could a dress designer be spurred to commit a crime because a design has been stolen? Could a professor kill because he lost his position or chance for promotion? Could an advertising agency try to murder the president of a competing firm? Could an actress do away with a professional rival? With remarkable uniformity (albeit with some exceptions) the answers to questions such as these are in the negative. Experiments with quirky motives tend to fare badly and throw the novel out of kilter. Amanda Cross erred in *Poetic Justice,* by making the motive for the crime unconvincingly academic and theoretical. In most detective novels, murder has deep roots that feed on man's sinful nature.

Deadly Meeting is illuminating on the relations between academia and crime, which constitute one of the main themes of the novel. Bill Stratton goes to the airport to pick up Dame Millicent, a visiting scholar who, besides being a distinguished medievalist, is also (under the name of Deirdre Desiree) an author of mysteries. Dame Millicent is a strange-looking, hard-drinking, dog-loving eccentric of the English school— and will, of course, turn out to be of great help in the murder investigation. As soon as Dame Millicent arrives on the scene, she expresses in no uncertain terms her conviction that Jackson's death was murder:

> "Murder, I'm sure. It would have to be. And almost certainly by a medievalist. One who had read those articles of his. Sorry as I am to say it, they deserved murder. Yes, I'm afraid it was murder." (p. 109)

These remarks must be taken as facetious, since Dame Millicent's insight is later shown to be perfectly sound. Her literary expertise (of both kinds, high and low), far from obscuring her sense of reality, only reinforces it.

This connection drives home the point that the campus is a microcosm:

> The pain and exaltation that lived side by side on the campus were little different from those felt by the rest of the

world, either in intensity or in quality. The men whom he was to see in a few minutes differed little from the rest of mankind except in their intellectual interests. Hatred, lust, envy, avarice: they were as much a part of a professor's makeup as intellectual clarity, the dispassionate judgment of evidence, or the driving curiosity of the born scholar. Bill was more than usually aware of the darker side of the complex pattern of man. (pp. 94–95)

The interpretation of a professional milieu as a microcosm is indeed characteristic and is often presented in detective fiction. This interpretation is related specifically to the question of murder, without applying to less-than-basic matters such as social values, life-style, or professional ethics. Here again, Bill Stratton is explicit when he says to the police investigator:

Academics are a funny race. . . . Most of us feel more loyalty to our students than to the law. If you said murder, I think they would talk, but short of that, they would probably feel they were protecting the privacy of a friend and colleague. (p. 114)

The point here is that it is, precisely, a question of murder, which also completely legitimizes Stratton's double role. His status as colleague must yield, no matter how painfully, to the overwhelming necessity of finding the murderer.

Are "hatred, lust, envy, avarice" the usual reasons for murder? Separately and in a more or less pure state, they are not. They are more properly the stuff that classical comedy and satire are made of. Even hatred, which may accompany crime, is not self-generated and is not often the immediate cause for murder. In the motives for murder, among which greed and jealousy seem dominant, distortion and combination are constant. Greed becomes grotesque, lust is perverted by frustration, and hatred is often rationalized beyond recognition into a hybrid horror. Excess, in detective fiction, wears a hideous mask. Here again, as in classical

comedy, balance is a key to morality; even so-called virtue may
be converted into murderous motive. In *Take My Life*,
Fleming's main "weakness," anger, is unleashed by his
unbending self-righteousness.

Reverend Randollph and the Wages of Sin by Charles
Merrill Smith presents throughout contrasts between the
morality of some members of the clergy and other characters,
including, eventually, the murderess. Dr. Randollph is an
ordained clergyman whose profession is teaching, but who has
taken over the direction of a church for a year to oblige his old
friend, the bishop. He is a sophisticated, worldly detective, not
at all adverse to the enjoyment of the senses in his own life or
others', but ready, as all good detectives are, to sacrifice his
comfort for what seems to be his duty. In the course of the
investigation, it occurs to Dr. Randollph that the motive for
the murder may be an unconventional one, and it does turn
out to be so. Despite the religious trappings, the motive is
unusual only in the sense that it is the result of fanaticism (with
strongly psychoanalytic overtones). In other words, the motive
is not rooted where the police sought it: in greed or jealousy.

Like misers and lechers, fanatics are also favorite targets in
comedy and satire. But, just as the classical comic hero is
always blind, the murderer in detective fiction is always utterly
selfish. Selfishness is the function that accompanies whatever
other vice characterizes the criminal act. The immediate cause
for the main murder (when there are several) is often self-
protection and fear of discovery. Authors sometimes take
pains to establish this fact, especially if the motive threatens to
enlist the reader's sympathy. For example, in the Swedish
novel *Siden Sammet* by Maria Lang (translated into French by
Asa Roussel as *Cours . . . mon Aiguille,* 1966), set in the world
of dress designing, the murder turns out to have been
committed in connection with an illicit love affair. These are
dangerous grounds for a motive. But, just when things seem as
if the murderer had acted to protect his mistress, the situation
appears to be reversed. The real murderess was ready to see

her lover accused and punished for her crime. This sort of reversal is not uncommon. Some device must be used when the crime is connected with passion or jealousy, the legal category of the French "policier" called "crime passionnel."

A genuine "crime passionnel" is not an appropriate subject, and jealousy, just as it straddles comedy and tragedy and has been treated in both, is a two-headed monster in detective fiction. If the crime of jealousy does not also present an admixture of self-seeking baseness, it tends to disappear somehow in the final judgment. The murderer may kill himself, thus escaping the law (as in *False Scent*), or his intention to kill may misfire, in which case he is not a murderer at all in the technical sense. But the catharsis of bringing-to-justice cannot occur unless the criminal is guilty in some way of the additional sin of self-protection at the expense of others. The willingness to see somebody else accused of his crime is enough; this is what often happens.

If it is difficult to find the murderer, it is often not because the crime is clever or rare, but, on the contrary, because the motive may be so conventional and general. If "hatred, lust, envy, avarice" are as common on the college campus as they are anywhere else, the detective discovers that, in combination, they can be lethal. It is always with great relief that the reader sees his favorite characters exonerated at the end. However, too general a law should not be derived from this state of affairs; for instance, a moral platitude, such as "There, but for the Grace of God, go I," does not apply. Detective novels present fictional truths, which can be captured only in their existential movement. It is not valid to say that all of the suspects could be guilty, because they are not. The readers may often be glad to find that the murderer is a character that they found revolting from the start, but sometimes they must forego this satisfaction. Although it has the obligation to be discerning, justice is also blind.

What does this definition of guilt mean in our guilt-ridden age? It seems to give a practical answer to a Kafkaesque

obsession. Unironic and clear, it can be seen as a salutary
counterweight to the irony that underlies Camus's *L'Etranger*,
in which the hero Meursault expresses a diffuse sense of
culpability that has no connection with the crime he
eventually commits by sheer accident and perhaps in self-
defense, but has much to do with the verdict that condemns
him to death. An alien to his own guilt in a society whose
conventions he finds difficult to fathom, Meursault is a martyr
and a victim as much as a murderer.

Detective fiction destroys the duality of murderer-victim by
distinguishing between the two. Agatha Christie's comments
in her *Autobiography* are enlightening in this respect:

> It frightens me that nobody seems to care about the
> innocent. When you read about a murder case, nobody
> seems to be horrified by the picture, say, of a fragile old
> woman in a small cigarette shop, turning away to get a
> packet of cigarettes for a young thug, and being attacked
> and battered to death. (p. 529)

The haunting theme of "the wrong man" in several Hitchcock
films appears like a corollary to guilt in detective novels. From
The Lodger (1926) through *Strangers on a Train* (1951), *The
Wrong Man* (1957), and *Frenzy* (1972), an innocent man is
wrongfully accused and enmeshed in a web of accusations in
which his very innocence makes it particularly hard for him to
defend himself.

Detective novels address both our sense of guilt and of
innocence regained. On this point too Auden seems right in
"The Guilty Vicarage,"

> I suspect that the typical reader of detective stories is, like
> myself, a person who suffers from a sense of sin. From the
> point of view of ethics, desires and acts are good and bad,
> and I must choose the good and reject the bad, but the *I*
> which makes this choice is ethically neutral; it only becomes
> good or bad in its choice. To have a sense of sin means to

feel guilty at there being an ethical choice to make, a guilt which however "good" I may become, remains unchanged. (p. 158)

We may all feel guilty and suspect, but actual crime is not after all a matter for self-indulgent speculation. It is a social evil that must be uprooted if for no other than practical purposes. To the extent that this truth is reassuring, detective fiction does provide a reassurance: specific, demonstrable crime is empirically different from Original Sin.

7 Psychological Balance and the Morality of Distance

As justice is pursued in the detective novel, the complete personality of the murderer is ultimately no more than a necessary construct. On one hand, there is the realistic support: the crime, the clues, and the motives, which "reconstitute" the criminal; on the other, there are some glimpses of a character. How are these insights related, and how are they related to other characters? As an exercise in critical detection, let us take three openings of novels that have no specific relation to each other except for the fact that they were published between 1970 and 1972: *Elephants Can Remember* by Agatha Christie (1972), *Death at the Chase* by Michael Innes (1970), and Brett Halliday's *Count Backwards to Zero* (1971).

In *Elephants Can Remember,* Agatha Christie seems to adopt some contemporary techniques in the presentation of character:

> Mrs. Oliver looked at herself in the glass. She gave a brief, sideways look towards the clock on the mantelpiece, which she had some idea was twenty minutes slow. Then she resumed her study of her coiffure. The trouble with Mrs. Oliver was—and she admitted it freely—that her styles of hairdressing were always being changed. She had tried almost everything in turn. (p. 11)

Michael Innes's *Death at the Chase* is an orthodox detective novel leaning to the comic, but in which psychological portrayal seems effortlessly modern:

> When out walking by himself, Appleby commonly obeyed his wife Judith's rules. These — perhaps picked up from her American connections — could be summarized in the injunction, 'Go on till you're stopped'. When, on the other hand, he was accompanied by Judith, he still, after more than thirty years of companionable pedestrianism, made intermittent attempts to check her more obviously unlawful and even hazardous courses. (p. 9)

Brett Halliday's *Count Backwards to Zero* combines devices of detective fiction with those of recent thrillers:

> The first two days out of Southampton, rain was incessant. But gradually, as the *Queen Elizabeth II* swung south into warmer waters, the sea began to smooth out and the weather improved. This was the big ship's final westward crossing of the year. For the next few months she would be cruising out of Miami, and that was her present destination.
> Dr. Quentin Little, in a corner of the first-class bar, hadn't noticed the changes in the weather. He had eaten nothing since leaving England. He was drinking vodka gimlets.
> "Waiter," he said, indicating his empty glass.
> "Yes, sir."
> Little looked at his watch, staring at the figures until what they were telling him succeeded in penetrating through the vodka haze. With a ballpoint pen, he made a calculation on a soggy cocktail napkin.
> He had seventy-one hours to live. (pp. 11–12)

At first sight, the three passages seem strikingly similar. They create the illusion that they are taking place in the mind of the character on stage and constitute some variant of inner monologue, indirect inner discourse, or point of view. The terminology is not particularly important, but the differences that are implied from the start are worth pursuing.

In the passage from *Elephants Can Remember,* the author
is obviously trying to relate all the information that is offered
to the consciousness of Mrs. Oliver. "The trouble with Mrs.
Oliver was—and she admitted it freely . . .": Mrs. Oliver's
awareness and external observation coincide. But this
parenthetical statement also reveals the notion that there are
two different realities. And indeed, less than two pages later,

> Mrs. Oliver paused in doubt and then called for assistance.
> "Maria," she said, then louder, "Maria. Come here a
> minute." Maria came. She was used to being asked to give
> advice on what Mrs. Oliver was thinking of wearing. (pp.
> 12-13)

Within the space of the last sentence, the author leaps into
another character's mind, however briefly. This is not a leap
of faith. We see the hand of the omniscient author who can
direct Mrs. Oliver, Hercule Poirot, and any other character at
will, even when she tries to confine apparent knowledge to
what should be revealed at any given time of the novel.

Death at the Chase is much more rigorous. The quoted
passage is not exactly an inner monologue nor is it indirect
discourse in the sense that Appleby was likely to think literally
in these words. But in the narrative space it describes around
the character, no information is given other than what the
character could know and in a style that is used to express him.
The following pages in the novel confirm this impression.
We are within or "around" Appleby's consciousness and
witness what he sees and thinks.

In *Count Backwards to Zero,* we are, paradoxically, so
much within Dr. Little's frame of mind that distinctions become superfluous. Does the first paragraph present
the character's thoughts? Probably not—"Dr. Quentin
Little . . . hadn't noticed the changes in the weather"—but it
contains only information that is available to him, and it states
the situation in which he finds himself at present.

Questions of narrative technique and psychological description become doubly relevant in detective fiction, because it is a genre that is so delicately poised on its duality: detective and fictive. (In Agatha Christie's attempts to adapt her presentation to contemporary demands, the requirements of the short story lurk with their old vigilance. From the point of view of detection and for purposes of suspense, an ideal schema could be set out. We can sometimes share the detective's thoughts, but all other characters, being suspect, must be presented from the outside. This is, of course, a confining pattern. Some authors manage to conform to this pattern by reducing description to a neutral minimum and casting most of the novel in dialogue form. This pattern has its own efficacy, but it produces works that are psychologically thin)

Where psychological insight is important, the author has to use various approaches to illuminate character. Here again, Agatha Christie has experimented diversely. She often presents characters' thoughts, but suppresses some that are related to the plot. In the case of Poirot, this is consistently true. The famous *The Murder of Roger Ackroyd* is a tour de force in which the criminal is the narrator, who carefully follows the outside contours of his guilt throughout. In these devices, there is an unavoidable element of trickery that impedes novelistic exploration. A more developed fictional character must come to terms more fully with the problems of point of view and of reality both hidden and revealed. We have seen in Chapter 2 how intricately this web is woven in *Death Has Deep Roots* and in *The Daughter of Time*. What is called truth is part of a pattern in which the observer and the observed are integral functions. In contemporary fiction, consciousness is often "outside" as well as "inside"; external fact is also both inside and out. States of mind cannot be clearly separated from reality; they are part of it, as it is part of them.

Brett Halliday's kind of presentation is difficult to imagine in works in which the detective's inquiry is the fundamental process, except if the detective is the character in question. Dr. Little, in *Count Backwards to Zero,* is the victim who is the most fully drawn character in the novel. This works against the detective catharsis for special ironic purposes of its own. Empathy with the victim is bound to lessen our concern for the investigation, which can never bring him back to life. In detective novels, the victim, by definition, cannot be the center of an intense dramatic interest. The victim and the murderer seem to be placed on an axis of the novel, and symmetrically mark the outer limits of psychological presentation, the other characters being distributed in between.

Does this mean that the psychological presentation of the victim must be minimal? That is the solution adopted in some works. The victim may only make a fleeting appearance and be characterized by a few gestures and bits of dialogue. Or the victim may be dead as soon as the action begins and afterward only offer slight material for psychological reconstruction. In either case, the victim may emerge as a disagreeable, ill-tempered, or comic, or even guilty character who is kept at bay by external presentation, so that the reader has no impulse to penetrate into the mysteries of the victim's life and mind. The terrible irony of such a character's death is then purely moral, without psychological overtones. In *Cyanide with Compliments,* Professor Moreton-Blake feels free to banter about the garrulous Mrs. Vickers: "Why doesn't someone chuck her overboard?" When the poor woman is actually done away with, our impressions of her have not changed. Only the discrepancy between the velleity of her being a selfish nuisance and her death provokes horror.

This is by no means always the case. The victim may elicit a sympathy tempered only by his or her small part in the novel. While alive, the victim is not a strong character or one whose motives and thinking we are given much opportunity of understanding. Once the victim's character becomes, through death, a part of the reconstructive process of the investigation, it may become a subject of psychological interest and allow for shadings and complexity. As P. D. James expresses it in *Death of an Expert Witness:*

> It was the strangest part of a detective's job, this building up of a relationship with the dead, seen only as a crumpled corpse at the scene of the crime or naked on the mortuary table. The victim was central to the mystery of his own death. He died because of what he was. (p. 88)

But reconstructive movement interposes a distance that makes it impossible to share point of view in the immediate drama of an action going forward. The character can be shown only through the eyes of other characters, through their reactions, through the events that took place in the victim's life and after his death, and the detective's constantly modified understanding of all these discoveries.

In *Reverend Randollph and the Wages of Sin,* if the murderer is somewhat unusual, so is the victim. The handsome, wealthy woman was found dead and naked in the practice room of the church choir, of which she was a valued and talented member. At first, all the characters who are interrogated echo one another's opinion of her: a helpful, happy, and radiant person. Since no immediate family is on the scene, this loss has no strong emotional repercussions — until much later, when these effects are subdued by circumspection in the answers of former lovers and of the family. As Dr. Randollph (as well as the police and others) collect more information and impressions, the obligatory envious gossip comes up, puncturing the idealized blandness of the earlier portrait. But what finally emerges is an ambiguous, qualified, difficult-to-interpret image of the dead woman, which is further complicated by her diary, in which she frankly expressed her reactions and intentions.

The distorted poetic justice of the crime is an added irony in
the moral of the tale. It is murderous fanaticism, not the hand
of God, nor a jealous husband or lover, that killed the
licentious sinner, if that is what she was. What she "really" was
is partly mysterious and partly revealed, to the extent that
understanding and knowledge can throw light on human
conduct in its multifarious reasons and widespread
consequences. All these insights are carried by the current of
the investigation and are reflected in the detective's point of
view, which automatically establishes a certain distance, not
only of retrospection but also of detachment and intellectual
curiosity. Dr. Randollph is charming and in a sense dedicated,
but he is also coolly academic and determined to preserve his
bachelor's privilege of an uncommitted personal life.

The murderer, as we have already seen, tends to be a much
less interesting character. What is of dominant concern is the
chain of motivations that clues can reveal, since it is his crime
and not his presence that defines the criminal's function.
Characterization often does not go much beyond this function
and remains external. The novels by Maj Sjöwall and Per
Wahlöö highlight the problems that are inherent in the
psychological presentation of the criminal, especially when
social ideas underlie the themes. Psychological insight has
special poignancy in the melancholy anonymity of all the
characters' lives. In *The Laughing Policeman,* Martin Beck
and his colleagues discuss the description of a mass murderer.
This discussion (which serves several purposes in the action
and meaning of the novel) has important implications for the
approach to the mentality of the criminal:

> Melander turned the pages to a certain passage and read
> out: " 'He is probably under thirty, often shy and reserved
> but regarded by those around him as well-behaved and
> diligent. It is possible that he drinks liquor, but it is more
> usual for him to be a teetotaler. He is likely to be small of
> stature or afflicted with disfigurement or some other
> physical deformity which sets him apart from ordinary

people. He plays an insignificant part in the community and has grown up in straitened circumstances. In many cases his parents have been divorced or he is an orphan and has had an emotionally starved childhood. Often he has not previously committed any serious crime.' " (p. 95)

This medical portrait, which is similar to a police description, is a composite image that combines symptoms into a synthetic picture.

But how else can you understand a psychopath? What would the psychopath himself say? "It is not unusual for him to explain his actions by saying simply that he wanted to become famous and see his name in big headlines" (*The Laughing Policeman,* p. 96). The dilemma is stated succinctly: the point of view of the criminal is useless for understanding the crime. The gap is unbridgeable between the medical collection of signs and the inner meaninglessness that constitutes criminality. This idea may explain in part the fascination exerted by amnesia on authors of crime novels and horror stories. A victim of amnesia is often suspect in his own eyes. He cannot tell what crime is buried in the hole of his memory. In the detective novel, the bridge is the detective's mind, even if the cure, like that of the physician, is partly based on ignorance and must sometimes rely on symptomatology. There is a relation, however, between the psychology of the murderer and that of other characters in any given work. The world of the detective novel pervades all of its aspects, and criminals, to everyone else's greatest chagrin, are part of humanity. In *The Laughing Policeman,* characters are described with restraint and economy; a way of laughing, a gesture, an accent, and an unkempt red beard draw a portrait.

When an investigating policeman is presented, we share his frame of mind:

Nordin was in no way disappointed. He had simply drawn the blank that everyone expected. If there hadn't been such a scarcity of clues, this tip would never have been followed up at all. But he was not prepared to give in yet, and besides he didn't fancy the subway with its horde of unfriendly people in damp clothes. (p. 121)

We are able to understand Nordin's feelings, his reasoning, his intentions, and his mood, but they tend remarkably to the general — "he had simply drawn the blank that everyone expected" — and the collective, the familiar sensation of a rush hour in the subway. Indeed, the states of mind that are most often described are basic: fatigue, heat, cold, thirst, hunger, and depression.

Another tendency is to the factual. As noted in *The Laughing Policeman:*

[Kolberg] went down into the dining room and had dinner. As he sat there it suddenly dawned on him that he had in fact stayed at this hotel exactly sixteen years ago. He had been working on a taxi murder. They had cleared it up in three or four days. If he had known then what he knew now he could probably have solved the Teresa case in ten minutes. (p. 202)

This inner monologue is so close to what must be taken as fact that there is no division between the two — certainly none worth making. The tone is similar to what we find in Brett Halliday, but with the important difference that here only the detectives are shown in this way. There are, in this novel, several detectives playing roles that are more equal than is the case in many novels. Here, too, there is a tendency to deemphasize unique and single consciousness. Basically, the criminal may present a terrible resemblance to everyone else. The description of a psychopath that was given earlier in *The Laughing Policeman* continues:

" 'A person who is a psychopath can appear quite normal until the moment when something happens to trigger off his abnormality. Psychopathy implies that one or more of this person's traits are abnormally developed, while in other respects he is quite normal—for instance as regards aptitude, working capacity, etc.' " (p. 95)

The most decisive psychological difference between the murderer and the detective stems from the use of point of view in their presentation. If Agatha Christie has so often played on the confusion and sometimes presented the thoughts of the murderer, disguised or not, it is probably because psychological exploration is limited in her novels. In most works by most authors, the murderer is seen behavioristically: through appearance, dialogue, action, other characters' reactions, and especially the refraction of his motives in the investigative reasoning.

This is a key to the psychological outlook of the whole work. The existence of the murderer among all the other characters creates the necessity for suspicion; "generalized suspicion," as Ludovic Janvier calls it, affects all aspects of the detective novel. It works by a reciprocal system: characters are presented in a certain way because they are suspect, and they are suspect because they are presented in this way. This suspicion represents essentially the distance of subjectivity that is demanded by the implicit question: how much can we know about a character? The restrictions that this question imposes on the author vary considerably. There may be a certain hierarchy among the characters, which is reflected in the manner of their presentation. Minor or marginal characters may utter their thoughts quite spontaneously, as they wonder how to recognize a traveler whom they are to pick up at an airport, or whether their husband will come home in time for dinner, or how long it will take a steak to defrost for an impromptu meal. Since psychological techniques and approaches have evolved in literature, the authors of detective novels in the 1930s were less hesitant in revealing the inner reflections of various characters, especially at the beginning of the novel. Typically, the nucleus of characters who play a significant part presents a mystery, which echoes the mystery of the murderer's identity.

This state of affairs does not mean that psychological exploration must be reduced — it sometimes works in a contrary way. Curiosity may be enhanced, the necessity to link up the different parts of the investigation may act as a spur. Perceptive observers (detectives) are on guard against this very process, which threatens to form patterns where there are none, or it may blind them to the patterns that do exist. The modes of exploration are as diverse as the authors' styles, and they are also connected with the investigators' mentality. Clothes, gestures, and physiognomy are significant for some investigators, whereas intuitive gropings are the method of others. Moral distinctions may form a working hypothesis, and rational dialogue may be important.

In the detective novels of the 1930s, such as *Flowers for the Judge* by Margery Allingham, observation may quickly lead to inferences and generalizations:

> He was a fat young man with a red face, who looked less as though he had a secret sorrow than a grievance which was not going to be a secret very long. He regarded Mr. Campion with what appeared to be suppressed hatred, but as soon as the other ventured to remark inanely that it was a nice foggy day he burst out into the spasmodic but more than eager conversation of one who has been in solitary confinement.
>
> Mr. Campion, who thought privately that all young persons who voluntarily shut themselves up half their lives alone, scribbling down lies in the pathetic hope of entertaining or instructing their fellows, must necessarily be the victims of some sort of phobia, was duly sympathetic. (pp. 37–38)

Campion tended to think in categories, or at least to try to make sense out of immediate experience.

On the other hand, the Reverend Archery, in Ruth Rendell's *A New Lease of Death,* suspends judgment in his well-ordered observations:

> The man was small and dark and would have been good-looking but for his glassy, red-rimmed eyes. Archery thought he might be wearing contact lenses. He sat down at the Dufy table, ripped open a packet of Peter Stuyvesant and poured the contents into a gold cigarette case. In spite of the man's obvious polish — his sleek hair, svelte suit, taut bone-smooth skin — there was something savage in the way his white fingers tore the paper. A wedding ring and a big gold signet gleamed in the soft light as he tossed the mutilated packet on to the cloth. Archery was amused to see how much jewellery he wore, a sapphire tie pin and a watch as well as the rings. (pp. 68–69)

The observer may go further, even in his initial impressions, in interpreting the signs that confront him. He may not hesitate to draw objective conclusions when they seem obvious as in Margaret Scherf's *The Diplomat and the Gold Piano:*

> The arrival of one more human being, male or female, would not have been noticed by anyone, least of all Henry, if this one had not been of a different breed. He was a tall bony man, with a homely but good face, graying hair, steady eyes behind glasses. He looked very tired, and he was carrying a briefcase. To say that he was puzzled by what he found would have been to understate things considerably. He found Mrs. Cloche among the moving litter and went toward her. He had the look of a husband trying not to be hasty, wanting to understand, and holding in a tremendous indignation. (p. 13)

Nuances of distance, carefully weighted impressions, are quite easily contained in these initial descriptions. But matters become more difficult when characters are familiar, through long acquaintance or friendship with the detective, or through their prolonged presence in the novel. Then, dialogue, action,

interaction, reaction, realities emerging, and realities concealed, all constitute ways of deciphering character. How well
do we get to know the awkward young wife who has
inadvertently precipitated a disaster? Or the lanky, athletic
young man who has been smoking marijuana? Or the dirty-
looking, long-haired friends of someone's children? Or the
prim old maid with a white lace collar? Or the attractive
redhead who has been feeding and helping the bachelor
detective? We get to know all of these characters in varying
degrees, according to their importance and to the available
ways of understanding them. Some characters remain
shadowy and somewhat mysterious, whereas others come to
light. Limits of knowledge are set by the detective's point of
view, which filters almost all the facts of the novel. In some
novels, especially contemporary ones, the detective's point of
view may be overwhelming; that is, it may encompass all that
we can know of all the characters at all times. Sometimes it is
less rigorously maintained, although the basic situation is the
same. The point of view is often divided between two or more
investigators, each endowed with the power of self-revelation
to the reader. In *A New Lease of Death,* perspective is
established first in one mind, Inspector Burden's, although it
will later move away from him:

> It was five in the morning. Inspector Burden had seen more
> dawns than most men, but he had never quite become
> jaundiced by them, especially summer dawns. He liked the
> stillness, the sight of the little country town in a
> depopulated state, the hard blue light that was of the same
> shade and intensity as the light at dusk but without dusk's
> melancholy. (p. 7)

Inspector Burden's state of mind will soon include a
description of Chief Inspector Wexford, through whom in
turn we are introduced to Archery:

> In general Wexford disliked the clergy. To him the dog
> collar was like a slipped halo, indicating a false saintliness,
> probable hypocrisy and massive self-regard. As he saw it

vicars were not vicarious enough. Most of them expected you to worship God in them.

He did not associate them with good looks and charm. Henry Archery, therefore, caused him slight surprise. He was possibly not much younger than Wexford himself, but he was still slim and exceedingly good-looking, and he was wearing an ordinary rather light-coloured suit and an ordinary collar and tie. His hair was thick enough and fair enough for the grey not to show much, his skin was tanned and his features had a pure evenly cut regularity. (p. 30)

From now on, the central consciousness will be Archery. But he has initially been situated in another mind and presented from its angle. This is typically true of detectives. They are generally not the first person of the narrative in the main text of the novel (although they may be in parts of it). There are ways of imagining detectives through other points of view, through a full description, or through other external indications. We have seen in Chapter 4 that the portrayal of detectives is often gently ironic.

We are closer to the detectives and more privy to the workings of their minds than to any other character. Yet here too a certain distance is maintained in the psychological landscape of the novel. We are rarely permitted to go so far as to literally suspect the detective himself (although this is an occasional possibility). But, symbolically, "suspicion" operates even in our view of the main character. In the novels of Rex Stout, for instance, Archie Goodwin is the narrator, which curiously divides the figure of the detective. Thus, Nero Wolfe, the mastermind and body of enormous proportions, is seen, in his loving care for his orchids, his gastronomical delights, and his mannerisms, while we follow Archie Goodwin on his errands and in his reasoning. This device doubly removes both characters, one through the other. More commonly, the narrating voice is the author's—not the omniscient author, as in Agatha Christie's work, but the neutral tone endowed with life and color by the character which it is used to render.

The detective is a defined character tending to the "round," in E. M. Forster's terminology in *Aspects of the Novel.* We do not a priori share his values, unfamiliar as we may be with the ways of a clergyman, a lawyer, a banker, or a retired policeman. A priori, we only share the conviction that crime, and above all murder, is intolerable. Too close or too warm empathy with the detective is avoided; his peculiarities and special characteristics maintain the figure at a distance. Yet we follow his thoughts, and we share his impatience or his patience as we are taken into the spider's web, in the Jamesian metaphor, of his inquiry and his personality. This double approach with a built-in perspective is essentially social. It marks the limits of a novel in which psychological realities play themselves out on the stage of society. It is, in other words, the approach of the novel of manners.

8 Social Worlds:
The Microcosm and the Larger Reality

As in all novels of manners, there is a constant interplay in detective fiction between the customs and mores of a certain milieu and psychological and ethical realities. The murder is the breach that violently breaks open this microcosm and forcefully brings in the outside world. Even in the hospital, where death is a regular occurrence, murder brings a frightened hush and destroys the balance. What commonly happens in an English village, where the police seem part of the family, is that Scotland Yard must be called in. Scotland Yard is the medieval war alarm, the signal that the comfortable values of the town will be violated by rude inquiry, tactless probing, and intolerable suspicion. The fine distinctions of a society in which every member has his consecrated place will no longer be observed. The respected old butler will be interrogated with the youngest scullery maid and the masters themselves will be under more or less polite suspicion. The style in the conversations will change abruptly. The accepted small talk of tea parties — roses, fairs, the latest indisposition of Mrs. X's Pekinese — will yield to straight questions in an unfamiliar dialect or a neutral language that reeks of London talk.

In a small American town, the inspector may be a New York Jew, whereas among bankers under suspicion, he may be a stocky Irishman with a large family. In the world of advertising, he may be a down-to-earth skeptic with little patience for the frills of greed. The question of communication runs through the minds on both sides. Will the gruff policeman understand the delicate duties of the secretary of an important executive? Will he grasp how much a nurse can or cannot reveal about a doctor? Does he know how complicated is the matter of inheritance for a pair of stepbrothers? The policemen also may have trouble finding their way. Is adultery still a motive for murder among the fashionable rich? Do members of the jet set suffer from jealousy? How can a painting be worth millions of dollars? Why do people become so agitated about some old pages of manuscript left in an office drawer? Would a lawyer protect a criminal client? Are actors always playing a part, even in their private lives? Do scholars and writers care more about a real death than about what happens in their books? Would a bishop shield the wealthy trustee of one of his churches?

The gravity of the situation demands that communication be established. In *Deadly Meeting*, Robert Bernard shows that murder is the dividing line. Academic colleagues may not violate one another's confidence, except in a case of murder, which transcends the group's ethics. The detective may be the intermediary, and a policeman may have, so to speak, a social specialty. Maigret is an expert in the mentality of the *petit bourgeois*, or the worker, or even the petty criminal. He knows how to talk to people tossing down their morning glass of wine in a little suburban "bistrot" and he understands the quiet dreams of the Sunday fisherman, the bottled-up rage of the clerk under uxorious tyranny, or the morality of a "midinette" at a Sunday ball. We have seen earlier that some English policemen or detectives—Lord Peter Wimsey, Campion, Dalgliesh, and Alleyn—have their roots in the upper classes. The detective may also be a member of the milieu described in the novel (Bill Stratton, Thatcher, Rabbi Small, Dr. Randollph, and many others), who is helping the police.

By whatever means, the elements of the situation must become understandable and open to the investigation of the law of the land. This process of making understandable, of making us see, is symbolically that of the novel itself. The reader is also the outsider penetrating into an originally closed society with its own languages, manners, and morals. And although the action opens this closed society up and shows it to be a microcosm of society at large, it is still presented for itself as the scene of the action in its own particular colors and nuances. Sometimes we are jolted into awareness from the very beginning as in *The Unfinished Clue* by Georgette Heyer:

> It was apparent to Miss Fawcett within one minute of her arrival at the Grange that her host was not in the best of tempers. He met her in the hall, not, she believed, of design, and favored her with a nod. "It's you, is it?" he said ungraciously. "Somewhat unexpected, this visit, I must say. Hope you had a good journey." (p. 1)

Miss Fawcett is accustomed to her brother-in-law's rude ill humor, but the readers watching the curtain rise on this aristocratic country house setting have to readjust their expectations. The readers cannot smoothly glide into a scene of welcoming "Dahlings," drinks offered, or a polite butler's deft hand removing the luggage.

Forms are strictly observed in the host Sir Arthur's house. "But in spite of the fact that Sir Arthur's principles forbade him to quarrel on the Sabbath, Sunday had not been a happy day" (*The Unfinished Clue*, p. 40). Quarrels are contained, but they seem near explosion. Innuendos abound at parties about the general's much younger wife and his desire to disown his son from a former marriage. The seething of passions and conflicts reaches a high point on page 62: "really, it's more like a home for mental cases than a house-party," Dinah thinks. The English upper classes are often presented in this way. There is a crescendo of satire, constantly puncturing the outward forms observed by tight-lipped ladies, choleric army officers, and frivolous wives. Then, in turn, the satire is punctured as the investigation starts, and all the characters have to reveal themselves slowly through the traumatic events surrounding the murder.

Satire may be diffused throughout a novel, coloring the picture without being concentrated in any one part. Ross Macdonald often gives a haunting sense of southern California, and makes his satiric touches sharp but short. In *Sleeping Beauty*, for instance, every visit made by Lew Archer gives occasion for a social vignette. Real estate values (at least in their special, southern California signification) provide the first clue in the description. Then appearance, a gesture, or a reply quickly denote social status and habits. There are constant contrasts between the poor, the not-quite-poor, and the rich.

The action revolves around the powerful Lennox family, who have caused an oil spill that is threatening the beaches. When Archer goes to see the old William Lennox and his much younger wife-to-be, "an electronic gate had been installed at the entrance." Inside, there is a golf course and vast open fields with horses grazing.

> Then I noticed the woman standing inside the wall. She was wearing a riding costume topped off with a Mexican hat, and held a long-handled whip upright in her hand. She flicked it harmlessly in the air. (pp. 123–24)

Her hard, dark eyes reflect no feeling in the initial conversation, and only "softened as the mare came running up to her, hoofs drumming" (p. 125).

Archer's sympathies are drawn to victims of society, whose suspicion and evasiveness are only too well justified by their experience. Their surroundings reflect the hopelessness and helplessness of their situation, and satire is mellow and gentle in their cases:

> The pink house on Lorenzo Drive had a slightly abandoned look. The shrubs and flowers around it were either

overgrown or dying, and when I turned off the Cadillac's engine there was a waiting stillness in the air. (p. 135)

When Mrs. Sherry hesitantly lets Archer enter her home and he tells her that her son has probably been wounded,

> Shock struck her face a glancing blow. I guessed that she had been struck in that way many times before, and had learned the tricks of moral evasion. If you withdrew your spirit deep into yourself and out of sight, it couldn't be completely destroyed. But it might go blind in the internal darkness. (p. 135)

These short capsules of description are only initial presentations; later, satire yields more often to the ironic interplay of greed and envy, guilt and remorse, neurosis and illness, intermingling social classes, wealth, and poverty.

Prejudice often becomes a red herring in police discussions by pointing either to its victims or to its perpetrators, but it may be further interwoven with the social picture. In the small college where the action takes place in *Deadly Meeting*, there are powerful distinctions within the faculty of the department (and more specifically among the faculty wives). Bill Stratton's colleague and friend Tony Bongiovanni is of Italian descent and of modest means. He is justifiably and discerningly alert to snubs, especially those affecting his wife Laura, who is ill equipped to respond to discreet but overwhelming discrimination. The deep-rooted kind of prejudice, expressed in minute social matters, has little to do with professional status and power. A wife from a distinguished old American family may simply find that a headache tends to prevent her from accepting certain invitations. When matters of promotion and tenure come up, these social questions obtrude themselves and become of great concern. In *Deadly Meeting*, these questions become important in the criminal inquiry as well. Bongiovanni, as an Italian, counterpoints the dubious

Italian background of the victim, Peter Jackson. The two, of course, are not related, and, as we expect, types and clichés are exploded.

In *Tuesday the Rabbi Saw Red*, does anti-semitism in the little college where Rabbi Small gives a course have anything to do with Hendryx's death? It turns out to be irrelevant, but anti-Semitism undoubtedly had existed at the college. Mary Barton ("soon to be Dr. Barton") explains:

> "You know, when I came here in the fifties, it was the policy not to hire Jews for the English Department. Math, the sciences, economics, that sort of thing, O.K., but not for English. I remember they turned down Albert Brodsky. . . . Oh, he's the one who did that marvelous book on linguistics. . . . Professor Brodsky of Princeton? You never heard of him? Well, believe me, he's tops, absolutely tops, and they could have had him here, but then he probably wouldn't have stayed anyway. . . . Oh, yes! Well, what I was going to say is that they'd naturally be a little embarrassed, but they'd just pretend they hadn't heard. All except Roger Fine. He'd stand up to him [Hendryx]." (p. 171)

The question of whether Hendryx was an anti-Semite raises interesting possibilities. Rabbi Small says that he wasn't, but the impressions of other characters are less theological and more instinctive.

A parallel division occurs in the "Jewish feeling" among students at the college. Many of them take the rabbi's course in the hope of an easy grade and become rebelliously indignant when their academic misconceptions are pitilessly corrected. They needle Rabbi Small and often make things depressingly difficult for him in his new role as teacher. Yet when a student who is being interrogated by a police sergeant states the time at which the rabbi left his class on the day of the murder, he is rudely taken to task by a fellow student:

> "What did you have to tell him that for?"
> "Why not? It's a secret?"

"I don't see why we should wash our dirty linen in
public," maintained Luftig.

"Well, it just came out. Besides, since when are you so
buddy-buddy with the rabbi? You're always fighting with
him."

"So what? That doesn't mean I got to throw him to the
wolves."

"Who's throwing him to the wolves? Anyway," said
Mazelman, "don't worry about the rabbi. A smart cookie
like that can take care of himself." (p. 171)

Luftig shows an amusingly mistaken sense of loyalty to the
rabbi when he thinks that the rabbi is being threatened by
outside forces. Small's effort has been to counteract these
confused group feelings with rational enlightenment and
knowledge.

It is sometimes difficult, in the deep-seated emotions that
surface in the course of an investigation or a trial, to see where
alliances will be strongest. These conflicts are central in Zelda
Popkin's *A Death of Innocence*. This minor novel of manners
includes some elements of detection, although there is no
detective to orchestrate the themes and illuminate the
discriminations between social values. Marvin Hirsch, a
prominent criminal lawyer in New York, agrees to defend
Elizabeth Cameron, an airline stewardess originally from
Idaho, who has been arrested in connection with a murder.
Hirsch takes the case partly to oblige a colleague and partly
out of pique, when he senses that the Camerons (his client's
parents) are shocked to discover that he is a Jew. The
Camerons are modest Middle Americans; the father is a
pharmacist, the mother a former schoolteacher. They are
completely blind to their daughter's more than dubious
activities.

The Camerons' relation with their three children is
presented as a parallel to Hirsch's own family life. Several
ironies work themselves out. The accused, Buffie as she is
nicknamed, was utterly spoiled in her Puritan, teetotaling
home. Her independence concealed self-indulgence and

greed, and her popularity masked her indifference to her sisters, her parents, and her friends. Hirsch has his own troubles with his pot-smoking oldest son Johnny, who leaves home, and also his fat and overly shy second son. Are their problems the reverse of the Camerons'? Is Hirsch too demanding and too strict in his work ethic and his relentless pace? His children, raised in suburban luxury, seem ironically repressed and deprived, and the generation gap between Hirsch and his sons seems unbridgeable. More and more, however, the solidarity among parents attaches Hirsch to the case. His increasing sympathy for the suffering Mrs. Cameron, alone in New York, influences his defense and overshadows the initial contrast of the wealthy New York lawyer and the narrow small-town woman.

Mrs. Cameron bitterly sees the light, which brings her to the edge of suicide. Yet she eventually returns to the small town, where Buffie was everybody's darling, and to her mild and uncomprehending husband. Society realigns itself when the trial is over. Buffie, in her great passion for a paracriminal with a heartbreaking family history, has made her shabbily heroic gesture, which lands her in prison. Her guilt, presented anticlimactically, surprises no one. On the other hand, Johnny Hirsch comes home, tanned and strong after working in the fields all over the United States, but grateful to be back. His father also has learned to be grateful for his family's solicitude (as they have learned to feel concern for him). Johnny begins to respect his father because of his personal commitment to the Cameron case. What this commitment implied, however, may not be clear to Johnny. Toward the end of the case, Marvin Hirsch seems to have conducted the defense to satisfy Mrs. Cameron's need for justice. For her own release, she needed to see the law administer its full punishment to her criminal daughter. This final irony also works in two ways. Whether or not Johnny knew that his father had allied himself with Mrs. Cameron—whose new sense of justice, in turn, probably reflected her lawyer's—he basically approved of the outcome, since he had nothing but contempt for the ugly greed that motivated the crime. And Marvin Hirsch has learned to win by failing. "There are victories in failures too" (*A Death of Innocence*, p. 314). Of course, these are relatively small victories and small failures. Society rarely makes room for the heroic.

The varieties of heroic behavior are interestingly explored in *Johnny Under Ground* by Patricia Moyes. Emily Tibbett, Chief Inspector Tibbett's wife, goes to a reunion of former RAF and WAAF officers who had served together at Dymfield Air Base during World War II. A series of events occurs. Emily slides into agreeing to help Lofty Parker, a talented drifter, to write a biography of "Beau" Guest, a pilot and hero (secretly and devoutly admired by the youthful Emily) who had died in mysterious circumstances. What turns out to be an old murder issues into a new one, that of Lofty.

The novel flashes back and forth between Dymfield Air Base during the war and the lives of all those former officers twenty years later, after the reunion. There is also a third dimension: the legend around Beau, juxtaposed with the biography that Lofty and Emily are trying to write. Hildegard St. Vere Prendergast married Beau's widow Barbara, now expensively dressed and expertly made up. Together they lead a wealthy country life. Sammy Smith, "the ex-pilot who was the station's humorist" (*Johnny Under Ground*, p. 8), has become a car dealer, fleeing from his creditors and leading a shabby suburban existence. Annie Meadowes, married to a farmer in Scotland, looks like Mother Earth, "universal, mellow, and mature" (p. 59). Jimmy Baggott, the Radio Officer, "with his pockets continually sprouting screwdrivers and bits of wire (p. 8), is a famous television executive. "Dear old Arthur Price, the Equipment Officer," comfortably leads his homosexual bachelor's existence, cushioned by his considerable wealth. There is also the Reverend Sidney, Beau's father — and others.

These totally separate milieus interact through the plot, which draws the characters together again, but their relation to the past seems the more important theme. Life at Dymfield could be thought of as a daily give-and-take of heroism, or self-sacrifice and cooperation, with its own hierarchical structure and its ambitions, passions, and intrigues. Beau had died twenty years earlier in the halo surrounding that world. But how are the current concerns of the characters who had led that life connected with it? Is there a complete non sequitur between the heroic pilot and the car salesman? Or between the beautiful wife of the war hero and the rich, middle-aged matron with clawlike nails?

As more relations are established or revealed, a certain time-bound continuity appears, constituted by the characters themselves. There are considerable differences between the social values of Dymfield and the various ones that are prevalent in the lives of the businessman, the television executive, or the farmer's wife. One of those differences is in the telling and another is in the passage of time. If told as lived in the present, Dymfield seems different from the hallowed past. On the other hand, Emily Tibbett, in her middle years, has a candor and a simple courage that are not incompatible with the picture of the young, hero-worshiping girl she once was. Nor is her inspector husband's life free from emergencies and dangers. The murderer had behaved during the war very much as he did in the present, living "on a legal knife edge" (p. 221). "Never could make a success of anything, not even secondhand cars," he says of himself:

> For a moment Henry looked down at Sammy—a pathetic, gay, amoral, criminal, kind, cruel, funny human being. A gallant pilot. A cheat. A murderer. An ordinary man. (p. 223)

What is ordinary in a given society? The social picture that fiction presents borders on psychological interpretation on one side and on history on the other. The "historical whodunit" can be seen as a variant of the novel of manners. When the novel is based only on historical information (disdaining the ways of romances and other such hybrids), political and social customs emerge more from abstract descriptions and analyses than from characterization. Political and juridical explanations may form the background, and the interrelations among characters may be inferred from events rather than being directly presented. *The Overbury Affair* by Miriam Allen de Ford is an interesting example. It limits itself impeccably to available documents dealing with the mysterious death of "Sir Thomas Overbury, ex-secretary, ex-protégé, and ex-friend of Robert Carr, Earl of Somerset — the favorite of King James I of England" (p. 5) in the Tower of London in 1613. The novel presents at some length the trials of the defendants who are arrested for conspiracy in the murder, in the course of which the methods and personal ambitions of Sir Francis Bacon clash with those of Sir Edward Coke, Lord Chief Justice and "father of the common law."

To set these trials and the case before the reader, the author initially proposes a hypothetical analogy that must strike us, already two decades after the publication of the book in 1960, as curiously prophetic of Watergate. It is as if, once more, life imitated art, and the seventeenth-century analogue projected itself into the future.

> To give modern American readers some idea of what this celebrated case meant to the informed public of 350-odd years ago, let us imagine an improbable but logical analogy.
> Let us suppose (waiving all political and legal inconsistencies) that today in Washington a top Cabinet member, who was also the President's closest personal friend, was charged, together with his beautiful and prominent wife, with conspiracy in the death by poisoning of the Cabinet member's own intimate associate — the victim himself having been a member of the White House staff. Suppose that mingled with the murder charge were rumors of adultery and fraud. . . .
> And finally, suppose the President himself was rumored to be an accessory before the crime! (pp. 5–6)

The author underlines, where relevant, the differences between the criminal procedures used in these trials and those
that would be acceptable in an English or American court
today, including certain customs such as running the trial
through on the same day without interruption.

As always in the novel form, everything seems related. Use
of evidence in the elucidation (or its lack) of the crimes;
personal, social, and political ambitions at a given moment in
a given context; temperament, degree of intelligence, kind of
intelligence characteristic of the king, the judges, and the
various accused; the poisons used or described, and the
properties attributed to them (and by whom); the social roles
of the characters at a particular time (and the changes they
are undergoing in the course of the action); and movements in
the relations between England and other countries, as
reflected in the intrigues of the Court, are all part of the total
picture that emerges.

The reciprocal relation of manners and nature presents the
same ambiguity as in most novels of manners. The author
states this theme toward the beginning of *The Overbury
Affair:*

> Some of the celebrated beauties of history would doubtless
> astonish and chagrin us if we could see them now; standards
> of beauty change, and perhaps Helen of Troy or Cleopatra
> would never had had a chance in Hollywood. But Lady
> Frances Howard seems really to have been a lovely girl to
> look at, by the standards of our age as well as hers. (p. 14)

The meanings of the tale transcend its historical forms and yet
are immanent in it. Similar paradoxes are proposed in the
crimes and punishments. For instance, "beautiful little Fanny
Howard" was guilty (of what exactly still seems in doubt, but
at least of intended murder). "And even so, one hates to think
of . . . [her] dying in the agony of cancer, mad, melancholy,
lonely . . ." (p. 118). These ironies become particularly clear

in the broader outlines of historical narrative, but the structure of detection itself is favorable. Reflection is made at a distance. No decision must or can be made on the fate of the criminals, since justice, for better or for worse, has already taken its tortuous course.

La Peste by Camus (1947) can be seen as the great example in modern fiction of a symbolism based on historical or imaginary analogies. The epigraph quotes Defoe, who assumes in his *Journal of the Plague Year*, that "it is as reasonable to represent one kind of imprisonment by another as to represent any thing which really exists by some thing which does not exist." Symbols are given in self-contained pictures as well as in their universal projections. Within a system of open and closed references, the city of Oran is presented in and for itself. And, as in a given society in detective fiction, order is restored at the end. But even as the sea sends in a salubrious wind and the city can open itself once more to its customary life in health, things are no longer what they seemed at the beginning. The microbe of the plague may be hidden, but it has been shown to exist and will reappear.

Similarly, in detective novels the normal order is revealed to have been, to a certain extent, an appearance. This is sometimes indicated symptomatically by the presence of a criminal disguised as a country gentleman in a peaceful English village (for example, in *Death Has Green Fingers* by Anthony Matthews, 1971). The disguise, successful at first, points to the possibility that all appearances may be disguises and that evil is hidden in unpredictable ways. Perhaps the initial semblance of harmony, convincingly presented as it is, could be an idealized image of a society containing the seeds of its own destruction.

9 The "Silent Life of Things" in Novel and Film

G. K. Chesterton's praise of detective fiction—it is "the earliest and only form of popular literature in which is expressed some sense of the poetry of modern life"[1]—has often been quoted. Like a prince in a fairy tale, the detective moves through the London streets endowed in his quest with magic functions and signs:

> No one can have failed to notice that in these stories the hero or the investigator crosses London with something of the loneliness and liberty of a prince in a tale of elfland, and that in the course of that incalculable journey the casual omnibus assumes the primal colours of a fairy ship.

Lacassin, who sees the "roman policier" as the great epic of modern times, endorses Chesterton's view, although he makes a distinction between theory and practice in Chesterton's works (see *Mythologie du Roman policier,* vol. 1, pp. 254-55). Here again, the difference between genres comes into play. The detective novels that have been considered bear little resemblance to epic or to medieval romance. The detective, whatever the genealogy of his type, does not appear like a hero or a knight. Other branches of the family—closer to Poe's Dupin, Leblanc's Arsène Lupin, Hammett's Sam Spade, and Fleming's James Bond—have inherited these traits. Magic has yielded to earthly charm and to a poetry that is very much of this world.

I am calling "poetic" the imagery by which sensations, impressions, and feelings are conveyed; the complex of stylistic effects that Flaubert brought systematically into fiction in the middle of the nineteenth century, the means by which "a landscape [is] seen through a temperament," in Corot's phrase, and those by which the novel, as Conrad conceived it, makes you "see" — the means that make us *see* not only in the light of understanding but in an immediate sense.

Things come into their own again in detective novels not only as clues, although this ambiguity may enrich their function, but, as Jacques Barzun calls it, in their "silent life," the life of a quiet country lane or of a bustling city street, of a border of petunias in a garden or a book-lined study in a small apartment. Things exist in a wide and diverse sense, pastoral or urban, big or small, man-made or natural, important or insignificant. A frosty glass of beer, horse chestnuts fallen to the ground on a Parisian street, a muddy walk in the English countryside, a terrace looking out on a sunset over the Hudson River, a blue fall sky over the Metropolitan Museum of Art in New York — a multitude of images suffuse the pages of detective fiction. These images are sometimes connected with the hedonism of the detective, but not always. They seem to reflect a sense of life and awareness of its texture and feel, inwardly or outwardly. The strains of a Mozart symphony may be as clear in the mind's ear (in *Death Takes a Sabbatical* by Robert Bernard) as the honking of horns in the street. When Rabbi Small takes a year off to go to Jerusalem (in *Monday the Rabbi Took Off*), it is his daily family routine that gives us the atmosphere of the city, rather than any sensational or sensory effect. The Wailing Wall, for instance, impresses the rabbi little, disinclined as he is to sentimentality of all sorts.

A particular environment, a profession, or a set of tastes and customs may play an important part in a detective novel. The smell of chalk dust hangs over the tired afternoon of a department meeting in *Deadly Meeting*. In *Poetic Justice* by Amanda Cross, a professor stepping out of her office into the large campus of her university in New York, looks with strong emotion at the tulips in bloom and the students sitting on the

steps of the library. The feeling of Cape Cod life around
Wellfleet, Truro, and Provincetown completely pervades the
novels of Phoebe Atwood Taylor. And the soft dampness of
English gardens sends its flowery whiffs through scores of
works.

These impressions may be particularly vivid in the course of
a journey or in a new place visited, and journeys, long or short,
are a frequent motif in detective fiction. This may be
vestigially the quest, the mission, or the adventure, on which
the hero sets out. But the uses to which this theme is put
distinguish detective novels from adventure novels and
thrillers. Although a detective may deliberately start out on a
mission (Lord Peter occasionally, or Henry Tibbett, or
Maigret), this purposeful movement is more characteristic of
spy novels and adventure stories. In detective fiction, the
crime often occurs while the detective is taking a vacation,
traveling, or visiting. In any case, his perception, awareness,
and enjoyment of things are not functional to the case he is
investigating. Whereas Sam Spade or James Bond seems to be
galvanized into amorous ardor, the appreciation of Scottish
salmon, or the enjoyment of ice-cold drinks by the hectic
requirements of the chase, the middle-class detective takes his
contemplative delights where he finds them.

The continuum for the detective seems to be life, either
private or public. Duty and pleasure, purpose and relaxation
are the rhythms of his life. Dawn may rise poignantly and
beautifully on a police interrogation (in *A New Lease of
Death*). Cordelia Gray, in *An Unsuitable Job for a Woman* by
P. D. James, mourning her partner, nevertheless sets out on
her first detective job alone and with alert enjoyment:
"Driving in happy anticipation through the sunbathed
countryside, the boot of the car carefully packed with gear,
she was filled with the euphoria of hope" (p. 44). But Nero
Wolfe devotes his loving attention to his orchids at a certain
time every day—to be disturbed only in the direst
emergency—and his gourmet meals carefully prepared by

Fritz are sacred rituals as well. We have noticed earlier the detective's tendency to ritual, which punctuates his life harmoniously. An epiphany may occur during a doctor's early morning walk to his hospital, an old lady's pruning her roses, a policeman's questioning of a suspect, or a detective's sleepless night. It may also occur through a train window, at a restaurant table, or on a Mediterranean beach, or arise from a golden whiskey at dusk or a strong breakfast coffee. But these moments of perception are clearly coaxed into existence by taste and rite, and weave their way in and out of the action. These moments generally compose a counterpoint to the action, within and without the criminal investigation.

The contrapuntal structure may explain in part why this whole perceptual and affective domain—the silent life of things—which has been increasingly rejected by fiction in the last forty years or so, has found a refuge in the detective novel of manners. An inherent paradox seems to justify its presence: a driving action designed to hunt a dangerous criminal is perhaps the best context to savor the passing moment. The ordinary world of things becomes important again without shame, its fugitive beauty being the price of murder and destruction.

Similar reasons may underlie the curious incompatibility between the film and the detective novel. As Lacassin shows in his discussion of Dashiell Hammett's work, there was an immediate affinity, an "osmosis" between "roman noir" and "film noir," which ricocheted into literature and the films of Godard much later (see *Mythologie du Roman Policier*, Vol. 2, pp. 5-27). Elements of crime, mystery, murder, and even detection are widespread in film, but the appeals of the classical detective novel are rare in cinematic form. "Agatha Christie was never as well served on film as her contemporary thriller writers from America," says Philip Jenkinson.[2] This still seems generally true, in spite of excellent films such as *Death on the Nile* (1978), a charming comedy of manners and travelogue, or the haunting *Agatha* (1978), an imitation of a

Christie novel based on the mysterious incident of the author's
amnesia that occurred at the end of her first marriage.

In *The Detective in Film*, a valuable study with numerous
illustrations, William K. Everson perceptively analyzes many
differences and clearly states a basic one:

> However, while enthusiams naturally overlap, the detective
> *novel* and the detective *movie* appeal to entirely separate
> bands of fanatical devotees. . . .
>
> Given the enormous scope and range of the detective
> movie (and, like the westerns, it is as old as the movies
> themselves), the highly critical and exacting requirements
> of the detective novel *aficionados*, and the entirely different
> standards applied by those who care little for fidelity to a
> literary school as long as Basil Rathbone is Sherlock Holmes
> and William Powell is Philo Vance, this book can obviously
> hope to satisfy no one faction thoroughly. Devotion to
> detective fiction is a life's work in itself, as is devotion to the
> movies. (pp. 3–4)[3]

This incompatibility may seem surprising not only in view of
the constant cinematic use of adventure and mystery material
but also because the film is ideally suited to render the
"thingness" of things and the atmosphere surrounding them,
and, in emotive and perceptual ways, to make us *see* before
all. The film may be much less able to produce the shifts that
seem so characteristic in the detective novel: from perception
to action; from reflection to meaning; from meaning to thing
and back again.

The 1974 version of *Murder on the Orient Express* by Sidney
Lumet, based on Agatha Christie's novel,[4] may serve as an
example. It is a successful film, yet its very fidelity to its source
underlines some basic differences in the effects produced by
filmic images and by language. The beginning scenes have a
special excellence: the hustle of departures around the
legendary, fashionable Orient Express, the characters arriving
one by one in their period costumes, all to be swallowed up in
the omnipresent train. There is restraint, however, in the local

color — no undue insistence on detail, no self-indulgence — but we are already, from the first shots, in a world quite different from Agatha Christie's. A wealth of associations surrounds the images, some historical, some purely visual, some cinematic. The very name of the Orient Express conjures up other directors and films (especially the first version of the one we are seeing); the closing of doors and the departure of the train suggest a symbolism that is much more dramatic in the film than in the text of the novel.

From then on, the action will all be inside the train: the sleeping cars, the dining car, the compartments, and the corridors. The "locked room" is an old pattern of the detective story, but its use by Agatha Christie does not feel overwhelming. In a novel, place can be perceived more abstractly than immediately. We may *know* where the action takes place, but the language of the text may not reinforce this awareness or make it simply irrelevant. In film, place is pervasive. In *Murder on the Orient Express*, there is an impression of confinement throughout. Initially, this impression seems to create too much suspense for an action that is presented rather anticlimactically. Later, it becomes monotonous, as the camera moves back and forth between one car and another in a train stopped by snow.

What could be seen as the climax of the novel, Poirot's final exposition, becomes a good dramatic moment in the film, in which the characters reveal themselves. But this drama is achieved at the expense of the psychological reasoning, which is dominant in the novel. The film does not (and probably cannot) follow the logical intricacies of the text; the satisfactions of the reader's rational mind are thus much subdued, and viewers tend to wonder why they are being presented with all those explanations without the corresponding questions that precede them.

There is, furthermore, a whole set of effects arising from the history of film that tend to work against the literary connotations (although at some moments they blend interestingly). Hitchcock, whose notions of mystery are totally different from Agatha Christie's, is often evoked. Lauren Bacall, who plays her strident role convincingly and charmingly, is a far from anonymous figure who brings forth recollections of too many films, including those in which she appeared with Humphrey Bogart. The problem is reversed in Albert Finney's excellent portrayal of Poirot; there is no traditional association between the actor and this part. We have a plausible and interesting Poirot, but he is not at all *the* Hercule Poirot that readers have envisioned through dozens of Agatha Christie novels.

Where imagery, tone, and atmosphere are more important than detection and psychology, the film may achieve great success, as it does in Robert Altman's *The Long Good-Bye*. Here, Altman's distancing effects—the hazy hues; Elliott Gould's shambling gait; the disconnected dialogue; and fleeting images of trees, cats, and water—superimpose themselves on Chandler's novel and form a convincing and moving, tragicomic whole. But once such a world is evoked on the screen, it is difficult to leave it; it is difficult to step in and out of it. The silvery moon shining on a lake or the setting sun reflected in a California pool carries its own meaning on film. How can we go from there to rigorous deduction about the facts of a crime or to the distinction between truth and falsehood in the testimony of a witness?

Hitchcock's famous manipulation of setting, objects, and all manner of detail is charged with suggestion and irony: nothing is as it is, nothing is as it seems. The reverse is often true in detective fiction. A storm may not announce any disaster but a natural one, and a curtain flying in the wind only points to a welcome or unwelcome breeze. There is a world to return to after the chase is over and the case is closed. Perhaps Lacassin is right when he says that the social function of the "roman policier" is to "reconcile man with his world":

A modern form of epic, the "roman policier" does not help man escape, but helps him remain in his prison.

It is much more than a simple by-product of industrial civilization: it is one of the means of bearing it.[5]

This theory effectively answers charges of evasion and escapism that have often been leveled at detective fiction. It takes the balances of the genre into account without overemphasizing the larger social significances.

10 Sequels and Series:
The Reconciliation of Psychology and Myth

The reconciliation with the world, Lacassin says, takes place through the "equilibrium of mythical thought and rational thought." This is probably one part of the vast system of balances at work throughout the detective novel. There does seem to be a mythological component, especially in the figure of the detective. The notion of myth has been much used and perhaps overused. The hazy speculations that myth sometimes elicits may partly explain why Cawelti, in *Adventure, Mystery, and Romance,* replaces it by the idea of "formulaic literature," which seems to serve his purposes better. But for detective fiction that substitution is a serious barrier. The attendant problems of sociological, psychological, and literary definition become all but insurmountable. How widespread in popularity does a formula have to be? How does entertainment differ from literary enjoyment? What, beyond the critic's judgment of value, establishes the differences between formula and genre? What are the structures of a formula? What is the function of a formula in any given work?

Myth is often vague because its many possible forms, broken up into motifs, can emerge in various genres and with different meanings. Harry Levin lucidly defines such a motif in *The Myth of the Golden Age in the Renaissance:* "the generic feature that various myths have in common." He describes an Ur-myth of the golden age, which seems strikingly evocative of values cherished by many detectives, a myth with a

> unifying concept . . .: pleasure unabashed, as Tasso is at pains to specify. Each of the many different versions . . . seems to take place against the same setting: a pleasance or pleasant landscape, the *locus amoenus*. Such images were projections of ideas, skeptical and naturalistic in purport, fostering an emphasis on free will, an ethic of hedonism, a cult of beauty.[1]

To suppose that the myth in its integral form might be present in detective fiction would overstate the case.

But T. S. Eliot showed long ago how a modern novelist such as Joyce used the structures of myth in *Ulysses* to bring order to his creation. And there is indeed hardly an important writer of our times who has not sought mythical ideas to shape at least some of his works. Myth can be rooted in literature (the Bible, the *Odyssey*), but popular forms are diffused in various media. His later insistence on text did not prevent Roland Barthes from exploring, in his *Mythologies*, types, patterns, or masks that seem to express the social aspirations and tastes of a period. Other French writers were fascinated, during the 1950s, by such phenomena as movie stars and their special relations to the parts they play in a given film, in which a mythical dimension asserts itself.

Is there a Platonic image or pattern of the Detective behind and beyond the detectives of individual works—that is, in the sense in which Humphrey Bogart or Greta Garbo or Jean-Paul Belmondo are behind all their roles, or Homer's Ulysses is behind Leopold Bloom? Some historians of the detective story would probably be inclined to say so, but would differ considerably on his identity as they differ on the origins of the genre. Is the detective Daniel, who cleverly interrogates the elders in the tale of Susanna and the Elders? Is he a knight of the Holy Grail? Voltaire's Zadig? Vidocq, whose *Mémoires* inspired Balzac as well as Poe? Poe's Dupin? W. Godwin's

Caleb Williams, perhaps the first English detective hero, who triumphs through virtue and humility?

These are all red herrings set out by the artifice of historical detection. If there is a mythical aspect in the detective, it is for all practical purposes subsumed in the characters about whom we are reading and must be sought there. To the extent that certain statements can legitimately be made about all the detectives of the classical detective novel — about characters as diverse as the Reverend Archery, Rabbi Small, Lord Peter Wimsey, Harriet Vane, Miss Marple, Dr. Davie, and Lieutenant Shapiro — there is a generic resemblance, which we have seen refracted in various components of the works: psychological, structural, social, and moral. It is useful to see this resemblance as a self-perpetuating series of models which answer one another within the same genre. The type here is a more specialized form of the construct that can be found in all fiction and allows us to speak of "a character." The idea of character, despite what some French New Novelists would have us believe, is behind all character, no matter how fragmentary. And, diverse as they are in language, history, or meaning, all fictional characters are in some sense comparable, just as all tragic heroes are, as well as all the gods and goddesses of the Greek Olympus.

Although some novels stand by themselves, there is a tendency to the proliferation of sequels and series, and detectives take on an existence that transcends individual works. Other literary characters have become myths: Hamlet, Faust, Falstaff, and others. But authors often endow the detective with purposeful permanence. This is eminently true of Agatha Christie's famous Hercule Poirot. The *New York Times,* on August 6, 1975, carried a front-page announcement of his death and mentioned the forthcoming publication of the novel *Curtain*, which Agatha Christie had written long before, in which Poirot dies. Hercule Poirot is dead, will die, has died; thereby, in these ambivalent statements, hangs a tale. Literary criticism has increasingly emphasized the notion that a character has no existence outside the pages of a book. This idea has been dominant at least since the New Critics in the United States and the New Novel in France, with strong reinforcements from structuralists and linguists. To conceive of a character as evolving in his own history is precisely the naive illusion that writers have been attacking most vehemently. Reality is the text, language its fabric, and Ulysses and Hercules are nothing but words.

The detectives do very often lead a life in the imaginary space between books of the same author. We start reading *No More Dying Then* by Ruth Rendell (1972) and find Inspector Burden in despair over the death of his wife several months earlier. A detective's child or children may suddenly play a part, or, like Martin Beck, he may turn out to be divorced. In *Johnny Under Ground*, Emily Tibbett is in the limelight, and her past during the war at Dymfield Air Base is reconstructed within the action of the novel. Some events in a detective's existence have happened in a time structure that is between the novels. Others can be assumed to take place in a paraliterary space in an earlier work, or decisive moments in the detective's private life may be presented in the work itself. Campion and Amanda are engaged at the end of *The Fashion in Shrouds*, as are Harriet Vane and Lord Peter Wimsey in *Gaudy Night*. Dorothy Sayers may have been the first author to face clearly the problem of her detective's chronological life, and this may throw some light on the development of the detective as a character type.

When Hercule Poirot embarked on his glorious career in detection, he was already retired in England, semidetached from worldly concerns and active life, private or public. He seemed to be cut out for a part in the Sherlock Holmes tradition. Without the intrusions of personal drama or turmoil, Poirot could be imagined to come back, inviolate, patent leather shoes and waxed mustache intact, in subsequent works. Campion, Alleyn, Dalgliesh, Grant, and

Lord Peter also appear anew in this way at different times. In a sense, these are mythical appearances: the characters are there, again and again, in their full assumed presence. After a certain number of novels, the authors felt the necessity to account for the detective's life independently. In other words, history had to be brought into myth; even Poirot had to become a character. In Poirot's case there were problems, because he was rather old to begin with — to his author's later regret his age has been calculated to approach 130 — and wise perhaps even beyond his years. Some authors seemed to find a new freedom in what may have been initially a burdensome obligation. Lord Peter develops into a moving character in his difficult courting of Harriet Vane, and detectives have become complex, full-fledged characters enriched by the new events of their history that are brought into each new novel.

Detectives have attracted biographies of various kinds. There is a heraldic history of a Peter Wimsey (which should perhaps be discounted in the interest of fictional truth), a biography of Nero Wolfe, and a character portrayal of Miss Marple. Authors themselves have been tempted into writing their detectives' biographical sketches, as in Otto Penzler's *The Great Detectives*. The intrusion of history into myth brings with it changes in meanings and techniques. The reappearance of characters that have become familiar through another novel can be used in the service of a special kind of realism, "visionary," as Baudelaire called Balzac's art. Critics have shown how Balzac introduced the "return of characters" in his *Comédie humaine*, and how crucial this device became. A whole cohesive society seems to arise from the pages of Balzac's works, as old acquaintances reappear, others do not, and people come and go in the flux. Similarly, Faulkner creates a world through the legend of Yoknapatawpha county.

In detective novels the whole, which may be the life of the

character or the society in which he moves, may function as a dimension of the individual works. This fictional creation or re-creation may lessen the typicality of the detective, not only by realistic characterization but also by the fact that the detective becomes a character among others. Here again, Dorothy Sayers may have led the way when, in *Gaudy Night*, she made Harriet Vane the central consciousness and also made her share detection with Lord Peter in a structurally more decisive way than Watson ever does with Holmes (or Poirot's helpers do for him). A neutral character in one novel may become a detective in another and vice versa. Ruth Rendell's Inspector Burden, for example, who is the detective in *No More Dying Then* together with Chief Inspector Wexford, was only a minor character in *A New Lease of Death*, where Archery took detection upon himself. In the later work Archery has disappeared. Thus, the fictional continuity that is established may not be concentrated in the individual characteristics of a typical detective. In a number of contemporary works, couples tend to be joint detectives, completely enjoying each other's confidence and taking equal risks, as in Anthony Matthews's *Death Has Green Fingers*.

This does not mean that the detective lacks the reflection of some mythical power or virtue, of qualities dreamt of and realized. Rather, these powers and qualities do exist, however much idealization is undercut by irony, however unimpressive may be a detective's vague gaze out of his grayish eyes, however unappealing his beer-induced pot belly may be. Sometimes the detective shares biographical traits with the author and is the author's idealized projection. More often still, especially in novels by women, the detective is an object of warm and protective admiration, of a love that is less Platonic than theoretical. We have seen how the point of view of Harriet Vane brings this dimension to the character of Lord Peter. The process may be particularly clear when the figure of the detective, as in Rex Stout, is divided: Archie Goodwin is free to idolize his master and to dwell indulgently on the foibles and strengths of Nero Wolfe's genius.

Whether the means, as in Rex Stout, are schematic, or subtle and qualified, the character of the detective in its mythical aspect represents a vindication of humanistic values: an equilibrium of psychological and moral forces, a role model for intelligence, taste, and the good life in a vividly imagined society like ours. As Raymond Chandler puts it, "If there were enough like him, I think the world would be a very safe place to live in, without becoming too dull to be worth living in."[2] Here again, the generic structure is complemented by the individual character, as psychology and myth are reconciled.

Conclusion

Throughout detective fiction, the interplay between the generic and the particular indicates the level of realism. The laws of the genre seem to echo the rules of a game, yet the gravity of the situations belies this association. The analogies that have often been given for the action of detective fiction are drawn from chess, particularly, or bridge — or the ever-present puzzle. These analogies are misleading, but they denote the play aspect of the works, which presupposes some structures, but creates new ones. Play combines freedom and need, and it takes place in its own space and time which become symbolically a part of it. Play is open, at both ends of the spectrum, to its own origin and reality that fuse with the surrounding world. Thus, it does not exclude myth or drama; it can include history, but also art; it is related to psychology, to literature, and to all the sciences that may come to mind. And, furthermore, it can turn back on itself and deal with its own existence.

The English language has a great advantage in being able to distinguish "play" from "game." In his seminal book, *Homo Ludens*, Johan Huizinga discusses other varied expressions in Greek, Sanskrit, and Chinese in connection with his idea that "it is probably no accident that the very people who have a pronounced and multifarious play-'instinct' [a reference to what Schiller called *Spieltrieb*] have several distinct expressions for the play-activity."[1] Whatever the pitfalls of philological reasoning, Huizinga's theories have great

relevance for detective fiction. Speaking of sacred play and
ritual, Huizinga quotes Plato's *Laws,* Vol. 7:

> Hence all must live in peace as well as they possibly can.
> What, then, is the right way of living? Life must be lived as
> play, playing certain games, making sacrifices, singing and
> dancing, and then a man will be able to propitiate the gods
> and defend himself against his enemies, and win in the
> contest.[2]

The moralistic import of Plato's injunction forecasts the
detective's moral tone, in which playful seriousness is an
indissoluble norm.

But Huizinga also warns against "overseriousness," which
has a paradoxical effect: "The virtue has gone out of the
game."[3] Play should not go too far or it ceases to be what it is.
The player may not "fall over," and the show must go on. The
mannered style of some detective novels, which maintains a
self-conscious distance between the events and the telling, can
be an excellent control. But there are many others. We are not
allowed to go too far into character, or into motive, or into
judgment, or into comedy, or into tragedy, or ideology. All
antinomies are balanced out: myth and novel; things and
persons; crime and punishment; past and future; art and
reality; psychological distance and proximity; history and
human nature; self and others; reason and feeling.

But if "the play's the thing," what is the thing that the play
is? The play sends us back to its being a play, that is, a genus
or a genre. If this is true of the detective novel, and of the
detective novel of manners, can one say that there are
meanings underlying its generic character? There seem to be
at least six assumptions on which the detective novel is based:

1. If reason or rationalism can no longer serve for clear
definition, detective fiction, nevertheless, asserts by the very
fact that it relies on them the powers of thought: by analysis,
intuition, deduction, or whatever mental processes. This

reliance also implies the belief that these powers are necessary. Whatever they are, they are all that is available.

2. Thought is seen as individual; that is, it has its source in one or several characters, even if they are, in some contemporary works, little personalized and sometimes close to anonymous.

3. Thought is — and it is socially necessary that it be so — communicable, at least for functional purposes.

4. Crime, whatever its reason, must be extirpated.

5. Society must be enabled to function.

6. Luck may be important in fate; no act or crime is reversible.

These few articles of belief in thought and society seem to be the smallest common denominator of detection, although they could be phrased or organized differently. These articles may explain in part why critics, following Régis Messac, have seen Voltaire's *Zadig* as a model for the detective story, not only because Zadig follows clues and reasoning in finding the thief who stole the queen's mare, but also because the assumptions about society and reason are close to those of the detective world.

This purely didactic substratum is far from reflecting the richness and complexity of the detective novel, and the discrepancy may demonstrate by the absurd what this study has tried to indicate. The genre of the detective novel cannot be defined adequately by a set of moral beliefs or by a series of rules such as those of a game. The assumptions are there, and rules or laws are observed, but what sets everything in motion is the life of the works. In other words, the detective novel should be read in its literary reality, not as a substitute for a game of chess or a point of law. Criticism of detection sometimes has distorted meaning by confusing it with assumption. Susanne K. Langer pointed out long ago (in *Philosophy in a New Key*) the importance of implicit understandings on the part of an audience or of readers. Similarly, a literary structure may be based on truths that are assumed, but go on from there toward its meanings. If a few elements of construction and morality were identical with meaning, there would be no need to read hundreds of works using the same elements. If hubris were the "key" to all tragedy, Sophocles, Shakespeare, or Racine need never be performed.

The detective novel has been vulnerable and has suffered many confusions, perhaps gladly; it is difficult to tell, but the suspicion arises sometimes. Many works are so self-aware and alert in literary matters that they seem to need no outside criticism, since they contain their own. Another fallacy that has often prevailed, here as in other literary forms, is the historical one. When a type, a pattern, or a theme, is traced to its source, the explicit or implicit deduction may be that the model and the evolutionary result are identical. But even if it were possible to establish a literary genesis with accuracy, its interest would still lie predominantly in itself. In a given work, what seems of main literary concern are the uses to which its material, traditional and original, is put.

Whether Zadig is the first detective of modern times may be a teasing question, but it has almost no relevance for the study of Martin Beck or Inspector Grant. Whether Alleyn's holiday in southern France with his wife and son is a residual quest from Arthurian romance can be debated, but it has little or nothing to do with the novel in which it takes place. The trip has much to do, on the other hand, with similar patterns of voyage, holiday, discovery, and coincidence in the lives of other detectives in the same tradition. A reading in the generic context gives the motif a relative, rather than an absolute, significance. Similarly, interpretation is inflected by the knowledge that the detective is conceived to be morally right. In what special ways? In what milieu? Why? And how? That is the individual province of a particular work.

Here my own defense must rest. The method used in this book is an experiment in a morphological or structural approach. The attempt has been to steer a course between historical and normative criticism. But other fallacies may not have been avoided, especially that the fine forms and shadings of individual works may no longer be discernible since they are seen against the superstructure of the detective novel of manners, which is itself a generic abstraction. The hope can only be that this vision is justified by the nature of the works examined. Detective novels are written in this dual, self-conscious perspective, and I am proposing a reading of the same kind. The purpose, simply, has been to clarify and qualify the question as to what detective novels might mean, as they have been written since about 1920 and are still being written and read today; what they mean, that is, as a literary form, and not in their psychoanalytic and sociological implications. I have borrowed methods that the genre itself suggests and tried to heed its warnings against guilt by association; foregone conclusions; confusion of almost identical facts; a naive belief in truth, historical or other; and confounding of intention and action, virtue and morality. In detective novels, every truth seems to be counterbalanced by a salutary doubt, and doubt in turn is counterbalanced by truth.

The special excellence of detective novels lies in the balancing of opposites and influences, in the delicate interaction of freedom and constraint. Where does this play of balances end? The play goes on not only in the particular work but from novel to novel in an open-ended sequence. And the sequence can issue forth into life, with which it is contiguous. There is play and play; there is play within play; there is young play and adult play (which may have different names).

The last notes of Josephine Tey's *To Love and Be Wise* eloquently take up this theme:

> As he [Grant] walked down to the bus stop a lovely mad notion came to him. . . .
> But of course he could not do that. It would be sadly unbecoming in an officer of the Criminal Investigation

Department; indicating a lightness of mind, a frivolity, that could only be described as deplorable in the circumstances. It was all very well for the Lee Searles of this world, people who had not yet quite grown up, to indulge their notions, but for adults, and sober adults at that, there were the convenances.

And of course there were compensations. Life was entirely constructed of compensations.

The fantastical was for adolescents; for adults there were adult joys.

And no joy of his "green" years had ever filled his breast with a more tingling anticipation than the thought of Superintendent Bryce's face when he made his report this morning.

It was a glorious and utterly satisfying prospect.

He could hardly wait. (p. 255)

Notes

Introduction

1. Michael Holquist, "Whodunit and Other Questions: Metaphysical Detective Stories in Post-War Fiction," *New Literary History* 3 (1971): 147.

2. Meir Sternberg, *Expositional Modes and Temporal Ordering in Fiction* (Baltimore, Md.: The Johns Hopkins University Press, 1978).

3. There is a brief but interesting discussion of these generalizations in Seymour Chatman, *Story and Discourse: Narrative Structure in Fiction and Film* (Ithaca, N.Y.: Cornell University Press, 1978), pp. 245–47.

4. *The Letters of Henry James*, ed. Percy Lubbock, 2 vols. (London, 1920), I, pp. 252–53, quoted by Sternberg, p. 297.

5. George Grella, "Murder and Manners: The Formal Detective Novel," *Novel* 4 (1970): 30–48.

6. W. H. Auden, "The Guilty Vicarage," in *The Dyer's Hand* (New York: Random House, 1948).

7. Gilles Deleuze and Félix Guattari, *Kafka: Pour une littérature mineure* (Paris: Minuit, 1975), p. 48.

8. John G. Cawelti, *Adventure, Mystery, and Romance* (Chicago: University of Chicago Press, 1976), p. 95.

9. Gerd Egloff, *Detektivroman und englisches Bürgertum: Konstruktionsschema und Gesellschaftsbild bei Agatha Christie* (Düsseldorf: Bertelsmann Universitätsverlag, 1974).

10. Roger Caillois, *Puissances du roman* (Marseille: Sagittaire, 1942).

11. Jacques Barzun, ed., *The Delights of Detection* (New York: Criterion Books, 1961).

12. L. A. G. Strong, "The Crime Short Story—An English View," in *Crime in Good Company*, ed. Michael Gilbert (London: Constable, 1959), p. 158.

13. Régis Messac, *Le "Detective Novel" et l'influence de la pensée scientifique* (Paris: Champion, 1929).

14. Ian Ousby, *Bloodhounds of Heaven* (Cambridge, Mass.: Harvard University Press, 1976).

15. Holquist, "Whodunit and Other Questions," p. 141.

16. Ludovic Janvier, *Une Parole exigeante* (Paris: Minuit, 1964), p. 49.

17. Arnold L. Weinstein, *Vision and Response in Modern Fiction* (Ithaca, N.Y.: Cornell University Press, 1974), pp. 15–16.

18. Auden, "The Guilty Vicarage."

19. Barzun, *Delights of Detection*, p. 10.

20. Julian Symons, *Mortal Consequences: A History—From the Detective Story to the Crime Novel* (New York: Schocken Books, 1973).

21. Ralph Harper, *The World of the Thriller* (Cleveland, Ohio: Case Western Reserve University Press, 1969).

Chapter 2

1. See, for example, "The Strange Nature of Pure Joy: The Historian's Pleasure Principle — 'The Psychiatrist, the Historian, and General Clinton,' " by William B. Willcox, and "The Pleasures of Doubt: Reenacting the Crime — 'The Limits of Historical Knowledge,' " by Robin G. Collingwood in Robin W. Winks, *The Historian as Detective* (New York: Harper & Row, 1968-69).

Chapter 3

1. Dr. Sarah Chayse, the psychiatrist in Lynn Meyer's *Paperback Thriller* (1975), is perhaps the most convincing, intelligent, and moving embodiment of psychoanalytic methods and ethics at work in detection.

Chapter 4

1. George Grella, "Murder and Manners," p. 34.

2. Ian Ousby, *Bloodhounds of Heaven*, p. 21.

Chapter 6

1. Francis Lacassin, *Mythologie du roman policier*, 2 vols. (Paris: Union Générale d'Editions, 1974), I, pp. 224-27.

Chapter 9

1. G. K. Chesterton, "A Defence of Detective Stories" in *The Defendant* (New York: Dodd, Mead & Co., 1902).

2. Philip Jenkinson, "The Agatha Christie Films," in *Agatha Christie: First Lady of Crime,* ed. H. R. F. Keating (London: Weidenfeld and Nicolson, 1977), p. 157.

3. William K. Everson, *The Detective in Film* (Secaucus, N.J.: The Citadel Press, 1972).

4. First published in England under the title *Murder on the Orient Express;* then by Dodd, Mead & Co. as *Murder in the Calais Coach,* 1934. My edition, the twenty-eighth printing, is called *Murder on the Orient Express* (New York: Pocket Books, 1940).

5. Francis Lacassin, *Mythologie du roman policier,* I, p. 18.

Chapter 10

1. Harry Levin, *The Myth of the Golden Age in the Renaissance* (New York: Oxford University Press, 1972), pp. xvi–xvii.

2. Raymond Chandler, "The Simple Art of Murder," in *The Simple Art of Murder* (New York: Ballantine Books, 1977), p. 21.

Conclusion

1. Johan Huizinga, *Homo Ludens: A Study of the Play Element in Culture* (Boston: Beacon Press, 1955), p. 29.

2. Ibid., p. 19.

3. Ibid., p. 199.

Fiction Quoted in the Text

The edition listed is the one from which I quote. When the date is considerably at variance with that of the first edition, I also give the original date of publication.

Allingham, Margery. *Flowers for the Judge*. New York: Manor Books, 1973. First published, 1934.

————. *The Fashion in Shrouds*. New York: Manor Books, 1973. First published, 1938.

Bernard, Robert. *Deadly Meeting*. New York: W. W. Norton & Co., 1970.

Borges, Jorge Luis. *The Aleph and Other Stories*. New York: E. P. Dutton & Co., 1978.

Butor, Michel. *L'Emploi du Temps*. Paris: Minuit, 1957.

Camus, Albert. *La Peste*. Paris: Gallimard, 1947.

Christie, Agatha. *Elephants Can Remember*. New York: Dell Publishing Co., 1972.

————. *The Labors of Hercules*. New York: Dell Publishing Co., 1978. First published, 1939.

Clinton-Baddeley, V. C. *My Foe Outstretch'd Beneath the Tree*. London: Arrow Books, 1974.

de Ford, Miriam Allen. *The Overbury Affair*. New York: Avon Books, 1960.

Egan, Lesley. *A Serious Investigation*. New York: Harper & Row, 1968.

Gilbert, Michael. *Death Has Deep Roots*. New York: Lancer Books, 1964.

Graham, Winston. *Take My Life.* New York: Doubleday & Co., 1967.

Halliday, Brett. *Count Backwards to Zero.* New York: Dell Publishing Co., 1971.

Heyer, Georgette. *The Unfinished Clue.* New York: Bantam Books, 1971. First published, 1937.

Innes, Michael. *Death at the Chase.* London: Penguin Books, 1971.

James, P. D. *An Unsuitable Job for a Woman.* London: Faber & Faber, 1972.

————. *Shroud for a Nightingale.* London: Sphere Books, 1973.

————. *Unnatural Causes.* London: Sphere Books, 1973.

————. *Death of an Expert Witness.* New York: Popular Library, 1977.

Kemelman, Harry. *Sunday the Rabbi Stayed Home.* New York: Fawcett, 1970.

————. *Tuesday the Rabbi Saw Red.* New York: Fawcett, 1975.

Lemarchand, Elizabeth. *Cyanide with Compliments.* London: Mayflower, 1973.

Macdonald, Ross. *Sleeping Beauty.* New York: Alfred A. Knopf, 1973.

Moyes, Patricia. *Falling Star.* New York: Holt, Rinehart and Winston, 1964.

————. *Johnny Under Ground.* New York: Ballantine Books, 1967.

Popkin, Zelda. *A Death of Innocence.* Philadelphia: J. B. Lippincott Co., 1971.

Rendell, Ruth. *A New Lease of Death.* London: Panther Books, 1970.

Sayers, Dorothy L. *Gaudy Night.* New York: Avon Books, 1970. First published, 1936.

Scherf, Margaret. *The Diplomat and the Gold Piano.* New York: Popular Library, 1963.

Sjöwall, Maj, and Per Wahlöö. *The Laughing Policeman.* Translated by Alan Blair. New York: Bantam Books, 1971.

Smith, Charles Merrill. *Reverend Randollph and the Wages of Sin.* New York: G. P. Putnam's Sons, 1974.

Taylor, Phoebe Atwood. *The Cape Cod Mystery.* New York: Pyramid Publications, 1970. First published, 1931.

Tey, Josephine. *To Love and Be Wise*. New York: Berkley Books, 1971. First published, 1950.

Woods, Sara. *Though I Know She Lies*. New York: Holt, Rinehart & Winston, 1965.

Bibliography

Allen, Dick, and Chacko, David, eds. *Detective Fiction: Crime and Compromise*. New York: Harcourt Brace Jovanovich, 1974.

Auden, W. H. "The Guilty Vicarage" in *The Dyer's Hand*. New York: Random House, 1948.

Barzun, Jacques, ed. *The Delights of Detection*. New York: Criterion Books, 1961.

Barzun, Jacques, and Taylor, Wendell Hertig. *A Catalogue of Crime*. New York: Harper & Row, 1971.

Boileau-Narcejac. *Le Roman policier*. Paris: Payot, 1964.

Caillois, Roger. *Puissances du roman*. Marseille: Sagittaire, 1942.

Cawelti, John G. *Adventure, Mystery, and Romance: Formula Stories as Art and Popular Culture*. Chicago: University of Chicago Press, 1976.

Champigny, Robert. *What Will Have Happened*. Bloomington, Ind.: Indiana University Press, 1977.

Chandler, Raymond. "The Simple Art of Murder" in *The Simple Art of Murder*. New York: Ballantine Books, 1977. First published in *Atlantic Monthly*, December 1944.

Chatman, Seymour. *Story and Discourse: Narrative Structure in Fiction and Film*. Ithaca, N.Y.: Cornell University Press, 1978.

Chesterton, G. K. "A Defence of Detective Stories" in *The Defendant*. New York: Dodd, Mead & Co., 1902.

Christie, Agatha. *An Autobiography*. New York: Ballantine Books, 1978.

Deleuze, Gilles, and Guattari, Félix. *Kafka: Pour une littérature mineure*. Paris: Minuit, 1975.

Egloff, Gerd. *Detektivroman und englisches Bürgertum: Konstruktionsschema und Gesellschaftsbild bei Agatha Christie.* Düsseldorf: Bertelsmann Universitätsverlag, 1974.

Everson, William K. *The Detective in Film.* Secaucus, N.J.: Citadel Press, 1972.

Gilbert, Michael, ed. *Crime in Good Company.* London: Constable, 1959.

Grella, George. "Murder and Manners: The Formal Detective Novel." *Novel* 4 (1970): 30–48.

Hagen, Ordean A. *Who Done It? A Guide to Detective, Mystery, and Suspense Fiction.* New York: R. R. Bowker, 1969.

Harper, Ralph. *The World of the Thriller.* Cleveland, Ohio: Case Western Reserve University Press, 1969.

Haycraft, Howard. *Murder for Pleasure: The Life and Times of the Detective Story.* New York: Appleton-Century-Crofts, 1941; enlarged edition, Biblo and Tannen, 1968.

_____, ed. *The Art of the Mystery Story: A Collection of Critical Essays.* New York: Simon and Schuster, 1946.

Holquist, Michael. "Whodunit and Other Questions: Metaphysical Detective Stories in Post-War Fiction." *New Literary History* 3 (1971): 135–56.

Huizinga, Johan. *Homo Ludens: A Study of the Play Element in Culture.* Boston: Beacon Press, 1955.

Janvier, Ludovic. *Une Parole exigeante.* Paris: Minuit, 1964.

Keating, H. R. F. *Murder Must Appetize.* London: Lemon Tree Press, 1975.

_____, ed. *Agatha Christie: First Lady of Crime.* London: Weidenfeld and Nicolson, 1977.

Lacassin, Francis. *Mythologie du roman policier,* 2 vols. Paris: Union Générale d'Editions, 1974.

_____, ed. *Entretiens sur la paralittérature.* Paris: Plon, 1970.

Levin, Harry. *The Myth of the Golden Age in the Renaissance.* New York: Oxford University Press, 1972.

Messac, Régis. *Le "Detective Novel" et l'influence de la pensée scientifique.* Paris: Champion, 1929.

Murch, A. E. *The Development of the Detective Novel,* rev. ed. Port Washington, N.Y.: Kennikat Press, 1968.

Ousby, Ian. *Bloodhounds of Heaven: The Detective in English Fiction from Godwin to Doyle*. Cambridge, Mass.: Harvard University Press, 1976.

Penzler, Otto, ed. *The Great Detectives*. Boston: Little, Brown, 1978.

Radine, Serge. *Quelques aspects du roman policier psychologique*. Geneva: Editions du Mont-Blanc, 1960.

Ruehlmann, William. *Saint with a Gun*. New York: New York University Press, 1974.

Sayers, Dorothy L., ed. *The Omnibus of Crime*. New York: Payson and Clarke, 1929.

Slung, Michele B., ed. *Crime on Her Mind: Fifteen Stories of Female Sleuths from the Victorian Era to the Forties. With a Descriptive Catalogue of over 100 Women Detectives, 1861–1974*. New York: Pantheon, 1975.

Sternberg, Meir. *Expositional Modes and Temporal Ordering in Fiction*. Baltimore, Md.: The Johns Hopkins University Press, 1978.

Symons, Julian. *Mortal Consequences: A History—From the Detective Story to the Crime Novel*. New York: Schocken Books, 1973.

Watson, Colin. *Snobbery with Violence: Crime Stories and Their Audience*. London: Eyre and Spottiswoode, 1971.

Weinstein, Arnold L. *Vision and Response in Modern Fiction*. Ithaca, N.Y.: Cornell University Press, 1974.

Winks, Robin W., ed. *The Historian as Detective: Essays on Evidence*. New York: Harper & Row, 1968-69.

Index